Advance Praise

I'm thunderstruck! Arlene Goldbard's new love-bomb-of-a-book—*In the Camp of Angels of Freedom*! What if, instead of spending all your time fighting off demons, you open up the doors to your angels? What if, instead of regretting all you shoulda, you acknowledge the overflowing sources of love in the education that is your very own life? What if you now take flight with these angels, free at last to envision a New Everything? All of which is grounded in your own experiences, your own life? Here is the path—fly!

—Bob Holman, poet, spoken word performer, proprietor of the Bowery Poetry Club, filmmaker, and host of *Language Matters*

. . .

Arlene Goldbard has written an absorbing tender and inspiring reflection on the extraordinary people who have touched, illuminated, and guided her. In doing so with such humility and generosity she has invited us to pause and consider how our myriad threads of human interactions contribute to the fragile fabric of human society.

—Gary Stewart, International interdisciplinary artist, Lecturer, Goldsmiths, University of London

. . .

I now know what it means to be educated in Arlene Goldbard's Camp of the Angels of Freedom. It is a story circle of gentle radical thinking that celebrates clear sight and truth-based compassion. I discovered more of my own story in its embrace, and my courage grew on every page. This book inspires and empowers with the forthrightness of the telling and the beauty of the stories told. Arlene is a master artist in the medium of the possible.

—Eric Booth, Founder, International Teaching Artist Collaborative, author of *Tending the Perennials: The Art and Spirit of a Personal Religion* and six other books

. . .

I've long admired Arlene Goldbard's work on culture and democracy. Her latest book touches on those topics, but it's driven by another passion, her outrage at the way education, which should be a social good, has become a profit center, and at the disrespect meted out to those with lived knowledge rather than formal credentials. She begins with entertaining and provocative stories of her own self-education, each chapter linked to a portrait she has painted of one of her "angels of freedom," individuals whose work inspired and guided her path as an autodidact. The writing is clear and accessible, her challenges to social assumptions well worth considering. I highly recommend her insightful, refreshing perspective on values and systems that influence all our lives.

—Judith Marcuse, LL.D. (Hon.) Artistic Producer, Judith Marcuse Projects; Founder/ Co-Director, International Centre of Art for Social Change; Senior Fellow, Ashoka International

Arlene Goldbard has trusted her curiosity, creativity, and character through a lifetime of self-education, always in the service of the common good. In words and paintings, she honours her guiding angels with love and insight, defending the human spirit that labours for a shared emancipation. I'm filled with admiration for its originality and her courage in creating something unlike anything else. Her story of a woman's path to wisdom is a training in fearlessness and a joy to read.

—François Matarasso, community artist and author of *A Restless Art*

. . .

The muscle in Goldbard's memoir and acute thoughts on education lies in how it prompts. Prompts via words and images that narrate a story of making place for oneself and us; that generate the power of autodidacts, angels, and imagination to figure our lives together. It not only prompts but it teaches how to walk through the world with honesty, curiosity, and a drive for social justice. The North Stars of belonging, culture, and possibility that illuminate this wonderful book show us joys, struggle, and beauty in freedom. This book is a gift of emancipation.

—Roberto Bedoya, Cultural Affairs Manager, City of Oakland, CA

In the Camp of Angels of Freedom offers important insights into the intersections of art, education, identity, and power in fresh, imaginative ways. I was struck by how Goldbard reimagines the wisdom of "her" angels in these times. This book is sure to provoke a great deal of conversation.

—Makani Themba, Chief Strategist at Higher Ground Change Strategies

. . .

I thought often as I was reading about how much I would have liked using this book in a course I was teaching on the sociology of art, on communities, or just generally introducing students to thinking about how private lives are structured by institutions, history, politics, and social class. I learned a lot from reading this book; it's beautifully written, carefully argued, truly a gift to the reader. I think it's a rare book that sticks in your mind for a long time after getting to the last page. That's my definition of compelling.

—Betty Farrell, former Executive Director, Cultural Policy Center, University of Chicago

IN THE CAMP OF
ANGELS OF FREEDOM

IN THE CAMP OF ANGELS OF FREEDOM

What Does It Mean to Be Educated?

• • •

Arlene Goldbard

New Village Press • New York

Published in the United States by New Village Press

bookorders@newvillagepress.net
www.newvillagepress.org

New Village Press is a public-benefit, nonprofit publisher

Distributed by NYU Press

Publication Date: January 24, 2023

First Edition

Paperback 978-1-61332-198-0
eBook 978-1-61332-200-0

Library of Congress Cataloging-in-Publication Data
available online at http://catalog.loc.gov

Cover image: Nina Simone by Arlene Goldbard
Cover design: Lynne Elizabeth
Interior design and composition: Leigh McLellan Design

To Rick, my heart, my rock

Contents

How to Read This Book

What does it mean to be educated? This book offers three different ways to make sense of a question that has infused my life and helped to shape every society.

Part One includes two ways of understanding, visual and textual. First, I offer eleven portraits of people whose wisdom has informed my own perspectives. Second, each portrait is accompanied by a short memoir describing how, where, and when I discovered that person's work, and how each affected my course in life. Third, Part Two features experiences and observations relating both to my self-education and to education as an undertaking in the current climate.

The essays in Part One lean toward the personal, highlighting moments but not telling the whole story of my life. Part Two engages the societal, but stories from both private and public realms are threaded through it. Together, I hope they offer a fuller truth, braiding the small scale of a single human life with encounters with generative, inspirational individuals and the wider sphere of educational aims and structures.

Life happens, many things at the same time. It is our task to give them meaning, to craft them into a journey. Each segment within this book stands on its own, side by side with something quite different. No experience or observation cancels another. I hope this will free you as a reader to take any path you wish through the book. You may decide to begin on the first page and continue to the end. But if you choose to read Part Two first, or dip into just one of the essays in Part One, or stare into the eyes of Nina Simone or Paul Goodman, then read a bit of Part Two before finding your next destination, I will not discourage you. To the contrary, *In the Camp of Angels of Freedom* is about the validity and pleasure of making our own ways through worlds of knowledge, including this book. Please make your path by reading.

. . .

In the essays in Part One, please note that the names of living persons have been changed to protect their privacy.

PART ONE

Angelic Encounters

Eleven Short Essays

Note to the Reader

The Hebrew word for angels is *malakhim,* which also means messengers. In Jewish mysticism, angels are messengers between worlds, translating spiritual energy from the highest realms to the earthbound, translating the earthbound actions of human beings to the worlds of emotion, intellect, and spirit. In contrast to humans, with all our contradictions and conflicting impulses, angels are understood as beings of single intention, bearing a concentrated essence.

Many teachers have proposed hierarchies and structures of angels. From them I have borrowed the idea of "camps" of angels, in which spiritual beings are united by a common focus. For example, the camp of angels of love might include an angel of brotherly love, of romantic love, of parental love, of patriotic love, and so on. Each of my eleven angels belongs to the Camp of Angels of Freedom. Each has been given a title and a singular quality expressing his or her essence. Each essay begins with the text appearing on that angel's portrait.

To me, spiritual texts and the stories and concepts they encode are not literal truth, but deep metaphor. I chose to depict the teachers whose works have guided me as angels because they have been messengers between realms, inviting me to leave ways of seeing that no longer serve and to enter a domain of greater awareness and complexity. Deep metaphor or not, I'm still a little superstitious—too superstitious, in fact, to portray a living person as an angel. While many people who are still living have inspired and guided me, I have depicted only those who are no longer alive.

These eleven individuals allow me to tell the parts of my story that shed most light on what it means to me to be educated. They appear in roughly chronological order, based on when I first encountered each person's work.

Making these paintings was a great pleasure for me. My way of painting is idiosyncratic, as with nearly everything self-taught. I found my path through trial and error, looking at work and leafing through books on painting mediums and the like. When I painted my angel portraits, I had a few aims. I wanted to honor each person with more than a superficial appearance. I wanted each person to meet the viewer's gaze in a way that invited more than a momentary encounter. Through both image and words, I wanted to express something about the qualities each had brought to my life.

There came a moment with every painting when the face began to cohere and I began to discern something beyond the surface. I knew when this moment had arrived because in each case, a feeling arose in my heart, propelling the same words past my lips. "Thank you," I said to each angel, and then "I love you." I felt sure each angel was looking back. Not everyone who sees the pictures will even know who all the angels are, just one among many reasons I can't expect the same type of love and gratitude to flow from each encounter. But I tried to imbue the paintings with that intention anyway.

I hope you feel something when you gaze into these angels' eyes.

1

Henri de Toulouse-Lautrec

*In the Camp of Angels of Freedom, Henri de Toulouse-Lautrec is
the Angel of Beauty in Ugliness, holding the quality of hopeless longing.*

The week I started this essay, I spent hours combing every bookshelf in the house for my big Toulouse-Lautrec book stuffed with color plates of paintings, posters, and drawings. It is so vivid in my mind's eye—the tattered sky-blue dust jacket, even the title page, where as a seventeen-year-old bride trying to make the best of my disastrous first marriage, I had written with careful penmanship the name that seemed to signal authority and possession: "Mr. & Mrs. Lionel G. A.—."

That book moved with me to the dozens of places I've lived since. I'd turned the pages so many times, they threatened to disintegrate. Where did I lose it?

To tell you what Toulouse-Lautrec meant to my young self, I need to share some of my story.

I was nearly two years old when my family moved to California. We all lived together: aunt and uncle, parents and grandparents, children doubled up in bedrooms, a boundaryless jumble, one in a row of stucco houses fifteen miles south of San Francisco financed by the post–World War II GI Bill. After a while, my parents and grandparents and my brother and I moved next door.

I was told the move was on account of a fight my grandmother and aunt had had over the proper way to make Jell-O. I'm inclined to believe it because, to my grandmother, Jell-O was a miracle drug. If I had a cold, I was given a mug of bright red melted Jell-O to drink. Gagging, I would choke it down. But surely close quarters bore more of the blame. My uncle and grandfather were both compulsive gamblers, the former addicted to cards, the latter to the track. The desperate scramble to wrest grocery money from their pockets on a winning day must have been amplified to the breaking point by the total lack of privacy.

California had its charms, but we did not feel at home there in the sense of belonging. Neighboring houses were occupied by families whose fathers had been mustered out after World War II, just like my father and uncle, choosing the promising new West Coast world. But my aunt and uncle were the only other Jews living nearby. Most of the neighbor kids went to the Catholic school down the block. Our family was different in obvious ways and in secret ones, and every part of life seemed to be contested. We had to go to the library while the other students sang Christmas carols; to be chased home by the uniformed Catholic kids when the pre–Vatican II catechism turned to vilification of Jews; to try to discover a bridge between my family's foreignness and the bright, shiny, real Americanism of our neighbors.

There were small and ordinary compensations. I was told that my father—everyone called him "Mack"—had chosen the newly built suburb where we settled by driving south from San Francisco until the fog stopped, a bright line in the sky. He loved to sit in the backyard on weekends, soaking in the sun, mopping his brow with a huge white handkerchief. Growing up poor in London's Whitechapel, he hadn't seen many oranges. Now he could reach up from his chair and pick one.

Where did I lose that Toulouse-Lautrec book? I must have been twelve when it was given to me. Five years before I escaped into the pretend adulthood of marriage to a college student whose addiction to drink came clear only after our shabby civil ceremony in the living room of my family's tract house. Sixty-four years ago.

Looking back at that part of my life, my anchor in time is my father's death in 1957. Mack passed away at forty-seven, about a month after my tenth birthday. I heard the story of his last breath so many times, I feel as if I were present when he drew it. It goes like this: My father, a housepainter, entered the hospital for a thorough checkup

to see if his fatigue had a serious cause. The doctors found nothing. When my mother came to pick him up, he was finishing a cigar. Getting out of bed, Mack turned to Esther to say "This is the last cigar I will ever smoke." Then he dropped dead. It wasn't discovered until the autopsy that one chamber of his heart had never developed. That plus a lifetime of hard labor and toxic chemicals led to his early death.

My own memory of that day is set at school. I was called out of my fifth-grade class and sent to the principal's office a few minutes before the final bell rang. My mother, my aunt Ruth (who lived next door), and the principal, who had previously seemed so steely—iron gray hair, starched white shirts, tailored gray suits, briskly clicking heels—all sat weeping. As soon as they saw me, Esther and Ruth rose and walked me to the door. Each gripped an elbow as we made our way to the car. I wouldn't get in until they told me what was wrong. At last, Ruth said it. "Daddy died today." My knees buckled. I flew high above the street. Tiny figures scurried far below. Then I was back in my body, we drove home, and my adult life began.

Art was my consolation. I'd always loved to draw, always been told I was good at it, especially at capturing a likeness. But my father's death was what made me an artist, and not long after that, Toulouse-Lautrec made me understand the freedom and challenge that identity might carry. Both stories are different, yet they are one.

Esther, my brother, Max, and I traveled to New York half a year after my father died. We visited a long line of relations, including cousin Ralph, who painted.

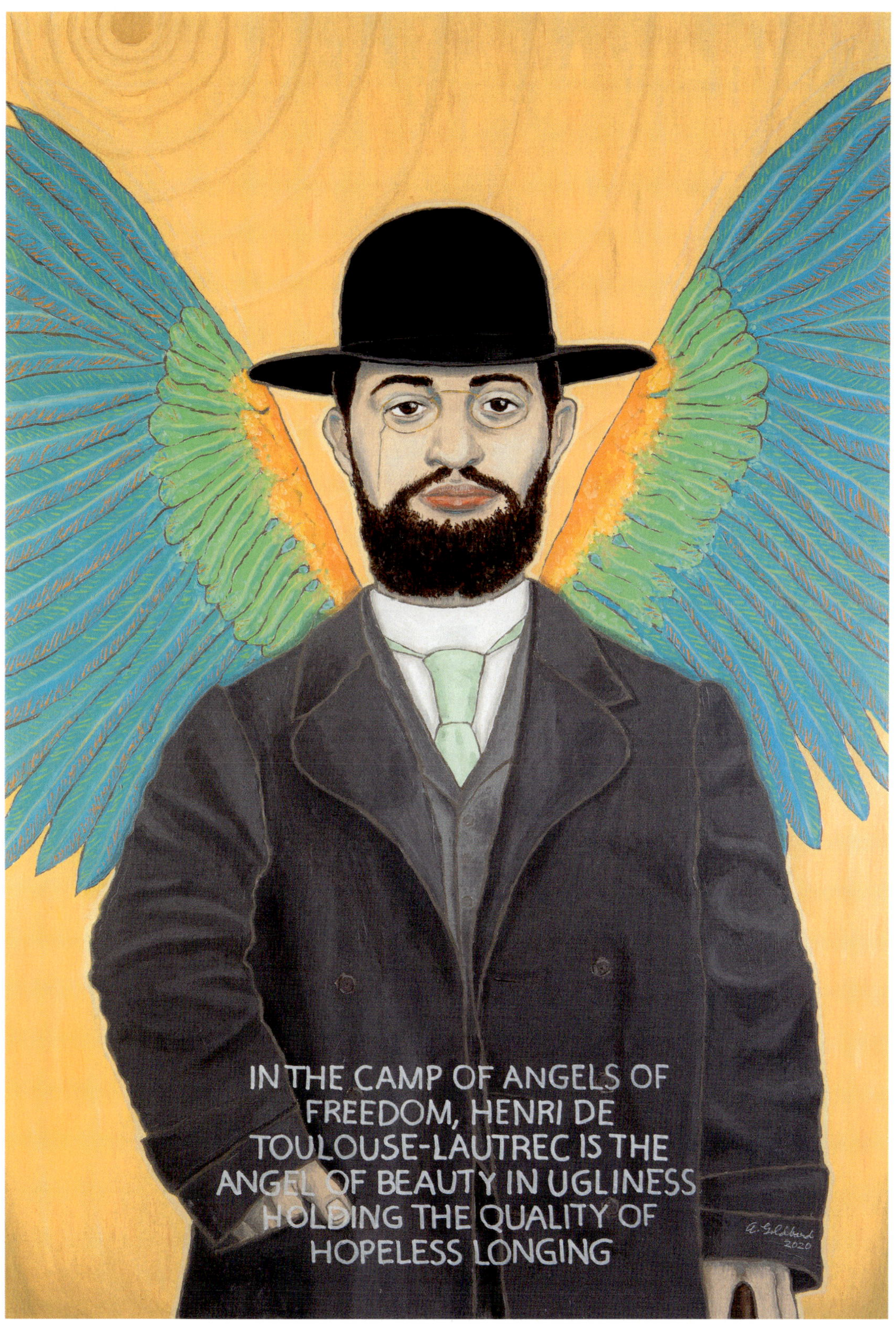
IN THE CAMP OF ANGELS OF
FREEDOM, HENRI DE
TOULOUSE-LAUTREC IS THE
ANGEL OF BEAUTY IN UGLINESS
HOLDING THE QUALITY OF
HOPELESS LONGING

While he and Esther talked, he set me up with a small canvas board, some paints and brushes. I made a painting of a potted plant—an aspidistra. I'd done plenty of crayon and colored-pencil drawings, smeared finger paints and tempera on endless pieces of paper in school, but this was the first time I had used oils. I wanted to do it again as soon as possible, and I found a way.

My family owned a cramped paint and wallpaper store on a small-town shopping street twenty minutes south of San Francisco. Until a few days before he died, Mack ran a painting crew out of the back while my grandfather worked behind the counter. Not long after Mack's death, Grandpa had a stroke. Then it became my mother's job to mix the paints and work the cash register. I went there after school to help, but if the store wasn't busy, I explored. In a clutter of forgotten things, I discovered a set of tiny oil tubes and brushes. I painted in a corner of the garage, always piled too high with old papers and junk to admit a car, let alone the battered blue paint-store van.

A year after the memorial journey to New York, we made another pilgrimage. My mother had never met most of my father's family, who still lived in London. The visit was challenging. There were many tacit rules. A young man who worked for my uncle was appointed to show us the sights. My mother felt uncomfortable sitting silently in the backseat, so she moved up front and made conversation, inviting the young man to lunch with us. When we got home, she was quietly cautioned not to be too chummy with the help.

But more than not knowing the rules, our emotions caused problems. The two of my father's surviving brothers and sisters who took turns putting us up had to endure loud and violent tantrums from Max, three years younger than I and perpetually beside himself with grief and rage my mother tried to stanch—and, failing that, to ignore. In the end, smiling through clenched teeth, the aunts and uncles sent us to a B and B the last night or two before we left England. When we checked in, we found a small pile of bills and coins on a table. It must have been a tip left by the previous occupant. This was a great relief to my mother (but surely not to the chambermaid), who had run out of money and could now get us something to eat.

I was older when I actually understood how little money my family had, how once everyone else had died or gone crazy, my mother had financed this trip and the rest of our lives with bad checks and a personal Ponzi scheme, piggybacking one credit card on another until they all ran out.

Before traveling home from England, we went on a ridiculous bus tour, a week in France and Italy. It was like one of those British travel comedies populated with quirky characters—some boring, some louche, some mysterious—and a noisy guide, a slightly shady stand-up comedian type. Each day ended with a *son et lumière* spectacle at a rambling château, usually enacting a battle. Paris was our last stop. My mother had the idea that it was the place to find things for artists, so when we got there, she followed through on a bribe she'd offered for good behavior, buying me a wooden easel that collapsed into a small suitcase. That made it official: From that moment I was an artist.

I first saw some of Lautrec's work in the museums we visited. I've since thought a lot about why a little Jewish girl in 1950s California identified so deeply with a physically challenged nineteenth-century French aristocrat. My family lived on the margins, while his parents were Comte and Comtesse de Toulouse-Lautrec. Lautrec was brought up in the ways of the aristocracy, then made art that rejected it; I had to discover social mores on my own, choosing those I wanted to adopt. His parents were first cousins, inbreeding accounting for some of his health problems. My ancestors were merely emotionally incestuous, unable to separate or differentiate in any fashion that might be considered normal. Lautrec's suffering must have been terrible. But art was his consolation, too. I think the connection has to do with my lifelong obsession with artists' ability to make something wonderful from their alienation, something of beauty and meaning assembled from the broken shards life had given them. Had given us.

The people Lautrec depicted—dancers, musicians, bohemians of Montmartre— lived amid squalor much brighter than my own world but familiar in its indifference to the rules of polite society, its shady dealings and socially marginal occupations. Lautrec made it luminous.

I was drawn to his paintings on pasteboard. Vibrant and mysterious, the colors seemed to hover over the dull mottled gray. I started to paint on pieces of raw Masonite, pressure-molded wood fibers creating an absorbent brown surface. I wish I still had the portrait I made of my mother's flamboyant and tragic friend Gloria. It was one of the paintings Esther placed in a shed in her backyard, telling me only that she'd stored them for safekeeping. By the time I tried to claim them, they were a mess of mold and cottony pulp. But this one lives in my memory.

Gloria and my mother had been friends for a long time—I think they met through the Jewish women's group Hadassah in the time before their lives fell apart, sitting on opposite sides of a card table set out for mah-jongg. Gloria had been a minor Hollywood starlet, or maybe just a chorus girl who had a few speaking lines. She'd married a prosperous pawnbroker and moved to a house in the hills with a pool, very glamorous and unlike any other place I'd seen. She was boisterous and sensuous, given to backless, open-toed pumps and plunging necklines, lots of chunky jewelry, and a perpetually full cocktail glass. In summer, her skin matched the mahogany furniture; I remember her saying she showered without soap to avoid spoiling her tan.

Tragedy stalked Gloria. Her youngest daughter, always vibrating with energy, was diagnosed a "blue baby," cyanotic from a congenital heart defect that 1950s medicine could no more repair than it could my father's stunted heart. After the child died, Gloria's husband killed himself. His death revealed far more financial malfeasance and debt than had ever been suspected. By the time Gloria and my mother morphed from suburban housewives into not exactly merry widows frequenting local bars, Gloria's circumstances were much reduced. In my first couple of years of high school, Esther was called repeatedly to Gloria's small apartment to pour coffee down her throat, to walk her around and around, trying to dispel the effects of not enough sleeping pills to be fatal. She brought me along to help.

I think it was out of gratitude that Gloria agreed to sit for me. I see her wearing a transparent nightgown—could that be true? The greenish cast of her complexion I borrowed from Lautrec's depictions of nightclub characters deep in their cups, slouching in pools of gaslight. I could tell from her expression that she didn't like being depicted that way, but to me it was beautiful.

And that is what I understood from Lautrec. Pauper or aristocrat, life takes you. If you are lucky, art takes you. I love the aphorism "Freedom is what you do with what's been done to you." It is the lesson I carry from Henri-Marie-Raymond de Toulouse-Lautrec-Monfa, who in his thirty-six years captured a world of yearning—of excess amid deprivation and deprivation amid excess—that ignited my own longing, and showed me where it might lead.

2

James Baldwin

*In the Camp of Angels of Freedom, James Baldwin is the Angel of
Seeing to the Heart of the Matter, holding the quality of fierce love.*

James Baldwin's 1962 novel, *Another Country,* was the first grown-up novel I read. I was fifteen. I loved to read, but by then I had tired of the bland young-adult books I could borrow from the library. I found it nearly impossible to relate to the volumes assigned in English class—*Moby-Dick, The Red Badge of Courage.* For all the virtues of such books, I now see that my class's reading list should have been labeled "Maleness: The Canon." Where were the pages that could teach me to find myself?

There weren't many books in my family's house, which was filled instead with the noise of three generations contending for breathing space. There was a recliner in the living room, and next to it on a round mahogany end table stood a lamp that now sits on my desk as I write. My father made it out of a tall Art Deco–style vase patterned with blue irises outlined in gold, the whole fitted onto a heavy brass base.

On a shelf beneath the table was a heap of magazines. Half were the women's magazines, such as *Good Housekeeping* and *Red-*book, that my mother liked to read at the dining room table while the radio or TV blared, dipping her hand with pistonlike rhythm into a bowl of nuts or crackers. The other half were skin magazines my uncle had brought from next door. I didn't know until I began to spend time in friends' homes that year that other people didn't keep such things in plain sight. I found them disconcerting and frightening—not so much the pneumatic airbrushed bodies as the line drawings that illustrated stories, wide-eyed young women in torn clothing looking back over their shoulders as they ran from a pursuer beyond the frame.

At the bottom of the pile, I found drugstore paperbacks that my mother treated like periodicals, discarding each as she went on to the next.

Another Country was a thick off-white Dell paperback, with Baldwin's name in large red capitals on the cover, and beneath it the title in black and a sketch of a man and woman embracing, facing a bridge. It looked dangerous and enticing, a long journey to an unknown destination. I picked it off Esther's discard pile and read it in clandestine snatches, in bathrooms and temporarily deserted bedrooms, wherever I found a bit of privacy.

It reveals something essential about my young self that my furtive activity was reading.

Usually no one took much interest in what I read, which was fine with me. Reading was associated with school, and when it came to school, I was on my own, no kindly supervision and homework help, as I'd seen TV parents offer their children. Yet even though no one was watching, with *Another Country,* I felt the need for caution.

Perhaps this was because the book confused me. My grasp of the facts of life was still tenuous. I'd been given a few horticultural metaphors—"the man plants a seed"—and heard some disturbing, if vague, rumors in school. Baldwin's text must have taxed my knowledge mightily. But it also gave me a glimpse of the life of the senses, and made me want to have sex as soon as possible, whatever sex might turn out to mean. The summer after I read *Another Country*, I got my wish, a childish affair with an African university student who'd been put in charge of a workshop I attended. He took me to his sister's apartment in San Francisco, and while we fumbled on the bed, his sister came home. Still, I gained an inkling of the information I was so keen to acquire.

Baldwin was my portal to the world of desire, its power and fluidity.

After *Another Country,* I read everything of Baldwin's I could find. I admired the graceful way he moved across genres, fiction to searing essays to plays. I was amazed by what Hasidic teachers might call his "holy chutzpah," the blaze of what Rabbi Abraham Joshua Heschel, another of my angels, termed "spiritual audacity." I was awed by Baldwin's seeming fearlessness in the face of ignorance, of willful stupidity and vicious indifference. I was inspired by the freedom his life embodied, and also the responsibility, how he could seek respite from the racism of the United States in Europe or North Africa, how he seemed always to be drawn back to bear witness to the freedom struggle.

I think often of the use Baldwin made of love. This is from *The Fire Next Time*:

> Love takes off the masks that we fear we cannot live without and know we cannot live within. I use the word "love" here not merely in the personal sense but as a state of being, or a state of grace—not in the infantile American sense of being made happy but in the tough and universal sense of quest and daring and growth.

I am still in awe of his love. I know how to love, but my love is almost always directed to a known heart, a known face, a known touch. I would like to be a person who feels that fierce love for . . . who? Humanity, nature, my people, my gender?

I see it all the time on social media, friends declaring "I love Black women!" or extolling *Ahavat Yisroel,* love for fellow Jews. But every human category includes people who extend themselves to heal or help and others who seek to do harm. No category of belonging inoculates its members against embodying envy or resentment, bitter revenge or misdirected fury, states of being I am unable to meet

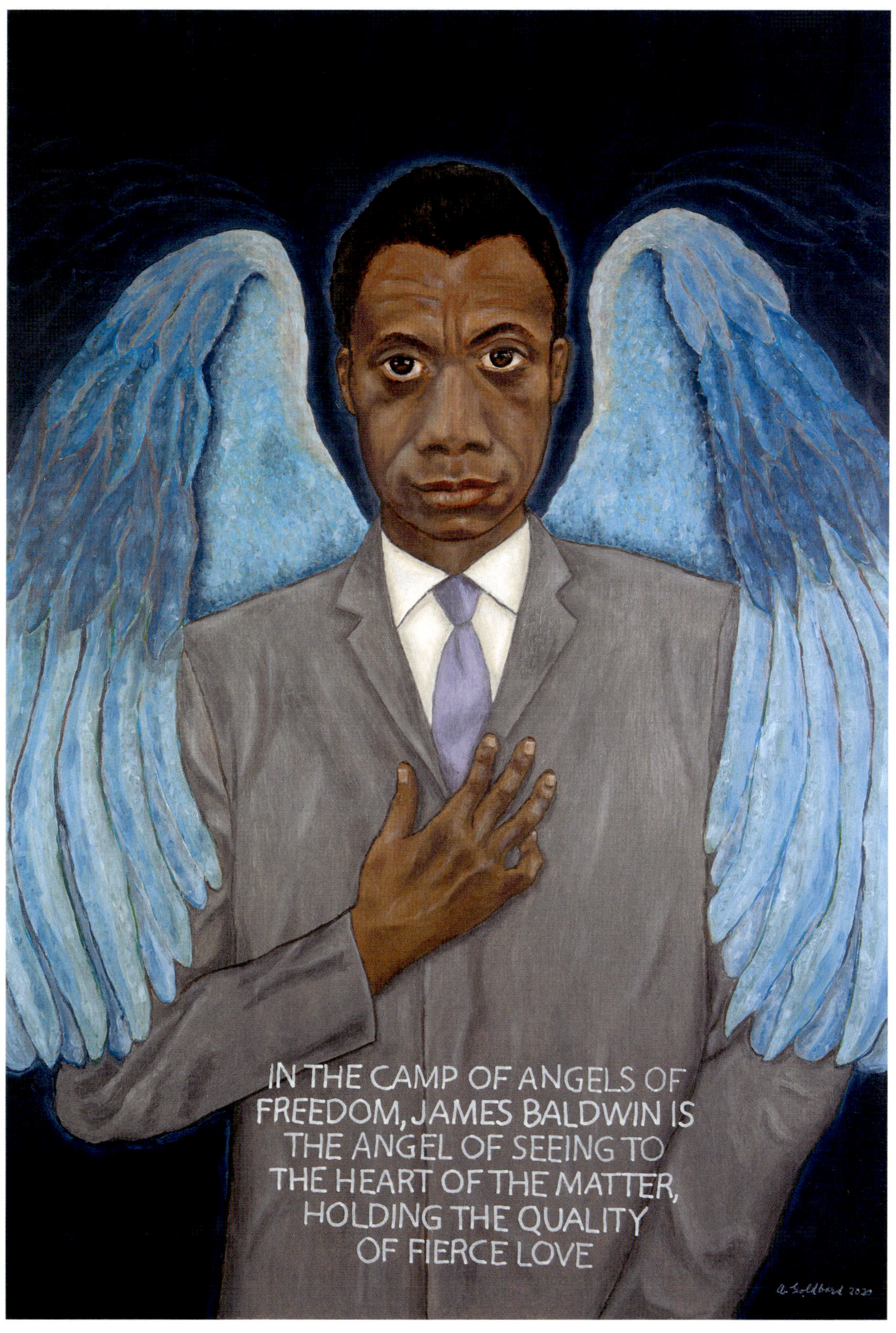
IN THE CAMP OF ANGELS OF
FREEDOM, JAMES BALDWIN IS
THE ANGEL OF SEEING TO
THE HEART OF THE MATTER,
HOLDING THE QUALITY
OF FIERCE LOVE

with love, whether in myself or others. My feeling for autodidacts comes closest. Belonging to that cohort engenders fellow feeling, the love that desires only the well-being of the beloved.

But no matter how I parse the categories, I can't always get to the mighty love Baldwin expresses with such beauty and power. I care, I do my best to extend that caring, but I have a hard time getting my arms around the meaning of this radical, universal love. Often, the nearest I can get is awe at the determination and perseverance so many must summon even to inhabit their lives, a compassion for others that eclipses one's own pain.

Baldwin's love daunts me. By daring to love and believing in redemption despite it all—despite it all!—Baldwin allows me to see that the fault lies within myself. I am still trying to repair it. I've been writing to repair it.

I first encountered Baldwin's work when I started high school, facing the stark choice between trying to live up—or down—to ambient expectations or hacking my own path through default reality to the mysteries I knew were waiting. The impression left by his writing was more real to me than the everyday conversations, the posturing and pettiness of high school life. *Another Country* is about a jazz musician, Rufus Scott, who seeks love but finds despair in postwar racial and sexual contradictions. When my mind drifted away from whatever the teacher was saying—to me, most of it was one drone, a steady hum of irrelevancy—I saw Rufus standing on the bridge, lying in his room, or walking cold city streets, and despite the fate the novel

foretold, his presence reassured me that if I could hold out, something better might follow. I could not have said then that it was Baldwin's voice that persuaded me to reject the stories others told, the ones that made me smaller, more lacking, more other, lonelier. But since then, he has always been in my mind, a beacon pointing to love.

I've been told that we live three lives: the first, figuring out what we're doing here—more in the sense of an underlying developmental or spiritual task than of an occupation; then the life in which we accept, and, if diligent and lucky, complete that task; and finally the one in which we perceive and embark on a new challenge and opportunity. Baldwin has been my companion in all three: discovering my path of helping to repair the shattered vessels of our collective life, pursuing it despite setbacks and missteps, and, finally, understanding whom I am here to serve.

There is a Baldwin revival going on nowadays, with beautiful films and biographies, endless social media memes, and copious sharing of half-century-old talks and essays that seem as new as now—and in the fashion of the day, with commentators eager to make their bones by debunking their elders. The latter is the feature I like least about twenty-first-century American intellectual life. It reminds me of the turkey vultures I see on some dry New Mexico afternoons, circling a corpse in the hope of making it a meal. But I don't think Baldwin's contributions can be obscured by this carrion dance. "Love is strong as death," says the Song of Songs. I think it is stronger.

I reread *Another Country* forty years later. My second marriage was on the verge of collapse. I had recently studied with a rabbi who taught an ancient spiritual practice, a structured process of asking higher powers to intercede for someone in distress. The seeker recites psalms and prayers of protection, humbly requests aid, then waits for an assignment to arise in the mind. It might be almost anything: studying, writing, praying, singing, or any other practice that is to be performed wholeheartedly for a specified time.

Just before the High Holy Days that year, I decided to ask my deceased parents for help. The assignment I received involved visualizing them—I saw their young faces bending over my crib—and recording what I experienced each morning for several weeks. I wasn't very far into the assignment when I heard my mother's voice. "Why should I help you? You'll just forget about me." I could see her point. Other than lighting a *yahrzeit* candle each year on the anniversary of her death, I seldom thought of her. I asked what she meant. Every morning after that, her voice came through with the same message: "Go to the cemetery."

I planned to leave in a day or two to visit with friends in Seattle, to attend services and get some rest, but I couldn't leave without heeding Esther's voice. What I found at the cemetery shook me. Next to the graves of my father, grandparents, and other relatives, each marked by a simple bronze plaque set into the earth, was my mother's grave, which bore nothing but a small plastic label, already faded. My brother, who had inherited the entirety of her meager possessions, had failed to purchase a marker. With my aunt's help, we bought a plaque. I never heard from Esther again.

When I unpacked in my friend's guest room in Seattle, I was surprised to find a copy of *Another Country* awaiting me on the bedside table. I opened it on a key moment. Staring down from a bridge at frigid waters, Rufus curses God, asking this question: "Ain't I your baby, too?"

When I first read the book, my young life was different from Rufus Scott's in almost every way, but his words wound themselves around my misery like a second skin. Forty years later, reading them again, I felt the same.

From James Baldwin, writing about worlds so different from my own, I understood that art can be a bridge to empathy and understanding, spanning even the coldest waters. In his work, the distance between personal and political disappears. He taught me that the little stories of our own lives always open into the big story crying to be told. No one is really fearless, but Baldwin seems so, making plain the fierce love and desire that can overcome—that are all that can overcome—the wounds that goad us to retreat from vulnerability, from truth, from life.

3

Nina Simone

*In the Camp of Angels of Freedom, Nina Simone is the
Angel of Knowing One's Worth, holding the quality of no fear.*

At this vast distance from my own youth, high school students mostly appear hip and au courant, exquisitely attuned to every fluctuation in the zeitgeist. But for me sixty years ago, high school was a self-contained universe astoundingly indifferent to what lay outside, obsessed with the games and gestures that assigned everyone a place in its interior society.

Our high school was new, built to keep up with the expanding Northern California population inhabiting tract houses bought on the GI Bill. It had a prefab look, dull gray walls that could be moved to make one large room out of two smaller spaces. It was built on an arid rise not far from El Camino Real, the historic eucalyptus-lined thoroughfare that followed the Spanish missions from San Francisco south. School was in the flight path of San Francisco International Airport, so—as happened during mealtimes at our home in Millbrae—class discussion often paused while the drone of the engines rose and drifted away.

At the beginning of the sixties, there were three main student groups. The elite group was all-white, neatly groomed, preppy, interested mainly in one another and pursuits I found baffling: team sports and cheerleading, clubs that had secret handshakes or symbols, parties and proms. Then there were numerous middle-rank students, who seemed ordinary and forgettable to all but the circles of friends they sat with at lunch. I thought they hoped to survive by fading into the background. A few Chicano kids were part of this group, but apart from a small number of Jews, all the rest appeared to be white Catholics and Protestants. Then there were the outsiders, who came in a few flavors: the boys who kept slide rules in their shirt pockets and were referred to as "brains," alienated kids who aspired to be beatniks, older boys who'd been left back and slouched through the halls in their leather jackets, kids who by virtue of looks or attitude were deemed untouchable, and a few in the interstices between these categories, which is where I lived.

I knew I was other. I thought I knew what I wanted, too, dreaming of an artist's life that would be nothing like the one I was living. I was drawn to the glamour and freedom I associated with artists. I lived for the weekends, when I could take the bus to San Francisco to see a foreign film, or visit with someone who owned a turntable and records by musicians I'd never heard or who could flip a switch and tune into a jazzy FM station.

Like many children of immigrants, I had learned the customs of the country enough to help decipher and navigate ordinary reality, but not enough to fit in. I was drawn to the other oddballs, attempting to connect by trial and error—mostly error, often too embarrassing to venture further trial. For example, there was a girl in my class who was universally understood to be too odd to risk association with. She wore clothes from another era, voluminous skirts and tight-fitting cardigans, sometimes hats and elbow-length gloves, well before "vintage" became a fashion statement. It was rumored that she'd been a fashion model at thirteen and had somehow broken down under the stress, and was now rehabbing herself at our characterless suburban high school. She was odd, yes, but also elegant and a little bit above it all. She entered the school's talent contest, performing "Wouldn't It Be Loverly," from *My Fair Lady,* with a brio undisturbed by catcalls from her classmates. She was Jewish, too.

I accepted an invitation to accompany her to a museum in San Francisco. Her mother served us lunch first in the dining room of their spacious, quiet, modern house, then drove us to the exhibit. We came upon a portrait bust by the sculptor Joseph Epstein. Smiling, I turned to my

companions and whispered something very like the confiding observations I'd often heard in my family: "Epstein," I told them, "he was one of our boys." The atmosphere froze and shattered, stopping my breath. The excursion didn't last much longer. My error taught me something about social class. The working-class Jews I grew up with were keenly interested in the game of identifying Jews, especially celebrities who'd changed their names. Pride was the foreground; but those name changes carried an overlay of shame. My companions that day didn't speak of such things, and for a while after that, neither did I.

I already knew how my home life looked from the outside: a chaos of piled-up papers and dirty dishes; shouts in Yiddish, broken English, sometimes Russian; contradictory demands from whichever adults happened to be around. Except for what I saw on television, I had no idea what purportedly normal kids' lives were like. When I came home from school, I would say hello to my grandfather, who lived in a hospital bed in the front bedroom, silenced by a stroke. He suffered greatly with the discomfort of having been catheterized. I crossed my fingers, hoping he would not fling back the covers and repeat the frightening grunts and gestures that pleaded for rescue.

Money was extra scarce in the years following my father's death. But I was a growing girl. There were certain clothes favored by elite classmates—madras plaid was big in those days, sweater twinsets, A-line skirts and matching headbands. For me, dressing for school meant raiding my mother's closet the night before, with

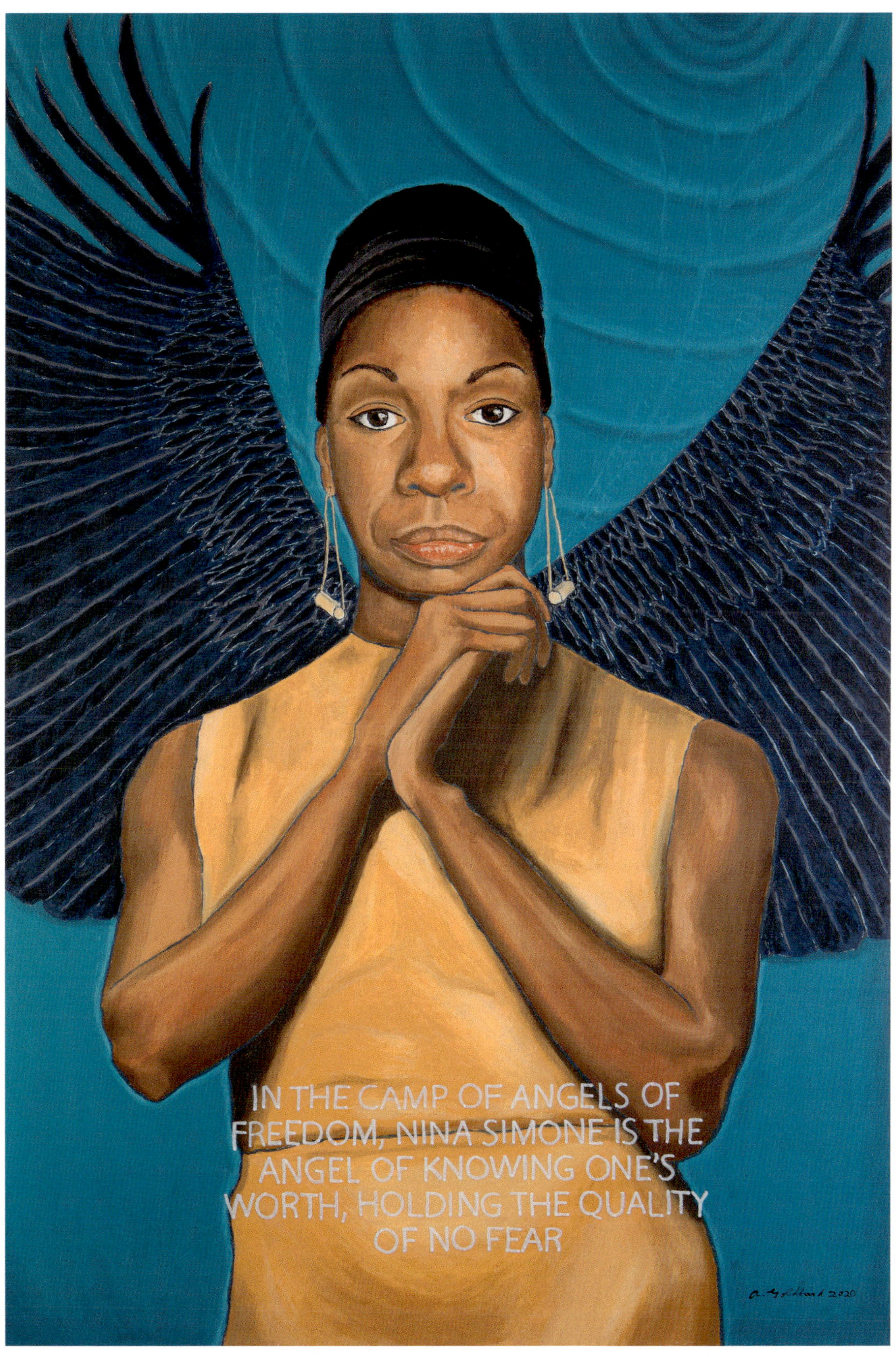

IN THE CAMP OF ANGELS OF
FREEDOM, NINA SIMONE IS THE
ANGEL OF KNOWING ONE'S
WORTH, HOLDING THE QUALITY
OF NO FEAR

no real idea of how my costume would be received.

When I met my friend Carla, I was wearing a long, narrow houndstooth skirt and a thin brown cardigan buttoned all the way up, a thirteen–year-old dressed as a cross between a late 1950s girl-group singer and a B-picture girl Friday. Carla was wearing one of the neat cotton dresses her mother ran up on her sewing machine. We couldn't have been more different, a slightly foreign-seeming girl with a trace of the immigrant accent inherited from her family and a very strange home life, and an all-American girl from California's agricultural Central Valley, newly settled in the Bay Area. But we bonded around shared otherness: People knew we came from someplace else—if not an actual territory, an alien milieu—just as we knew ourselves to be sojourners, merely passing through.

Carla teased me about my lunches— chopped liver sandwiches were renamed "green liver"—and I coveted hers, which included tiny paper boxes of raisins and neatly wrapped rafts of carrot sticks. She told me I said *orange* in the wrong way; I told her there was no *r* in wash. We liked Joan Baez and Bob Dylan (even though Carla's father imitated Dylan's nasal whine and told us to change the record). We read about nonviolence and schemed with a very few other outsiders to engage our fellow students in changing school rules. We tried to keep our faces blank when the PE teacher took us aside to say that wanting to be different was understandable but wearing black tights to school was taking it too far. We refused to participate in duck-and-cover bomb drills, and paid for

our audacity with time in the offices of our counselors, who were kind and knew when to pull out the tissues.

Carla's father sold insurance. He had a salesman's jokey demeanor and a temper that reddened his face. Her parents had grown up on farms, just a generation away from their Dust Bowl forebears. They worked hard to achieve upward mobility, and had been rewarded with their roomy suburban home. *Sunset* magazine was Carla's mother's bible. She and her husband listened to big-band jazz and went to sports car races at Laguna Seca, near Monterey. When Carla and I went to her house after school, we ate foods that were completely strange to me—marinated artichoke hearts fished out of little jars and piled on saltine crackers—and if her father wasn't home yet, we listened to his records.

That's where I met Nina Simone. Her first recording was released in 1959, the year before we started high school. I remember "Willow Weep for Me," "Wild Is the Wind," "Trouble in Mind," "Pirate Jenny," and, in our last year of school, Simone's own composition, the searing civil rights song "Mississippi Goddam."

Simone was a queen, armored in elegance. In Simone, I saw what I'd been stumbling toward, the first woman who seemed to hold a key to the life I longed to live. Now I see that same key belonged to every one of my female angels: self-determination undiluted by overmuch regard for others' opinions.

Her regal beauty and spirit were untarnished by circumstance. When I first encountered her music, I didn't know what a hardscrabble life Simone came up in as

Eunice Kathleen Waymon, the sixth of eight children in Tyron, North Carolina. I couldn't know what it was like to hold her reality and aspirations at the same time, but I knew my own. She studied to be a concert pianist and would surely have succeeded had she not been rejected from a conservatory, almost certainly on racial grounds. I didn't know then that she was abused by her second husband or that record companies and promoters slowed her career because they were wary of her politics. I didn't know the stories of erratic behavior and shaky mental health. Learning those things later only made me love and admire her more.

I just knew that when she sat at the piano onstage, upright on her throne, daring the audience to give her anything less than full, rapt attention, she was exacting her due. She knew her worth. I wanted to know mine, and I wanted it to be more than the paltry sum I'd been assigned.

Carla's house was a refuge for me. It was a long walk, but it was where I was headed on New Year's Eve in 1962, when I could no longer tolerate being cooped up in the house with my brother and grandmother, who had by then lost her mind. After my father and grandfather died, Grandma's life spiraled into a tighter and tighter knot. She had loved excursions, loved taking a special bus to Reno and receiving the pile of nickels that were given as a premium at the end of each ride, loved pulling the lever on the slot machine until her arm ached. Now she feared leaving the house. She believed she was being poisoned, refusing any food but cottage cheese and matzos, a diet she was unable to digest.

That night, terrified at my leaving the house, Grandma followed me down the street, beseeching me to come home in a voice loud enough to attract the attention of officers as we passed the nearby police station. A large uniformed man emerged from the station. As he walked toward us, we both snapped to attention, instantly on our best behavior. Surely Grandma was remembering the Cossacks who had killed her father, applying her early training in avoiding authorities' notice. For me, some type of genetic memory kicked in, a cellular-level fear and avoidance of the police I must have inherited at birth. It has never left me.

We walked home in silence. While Max and I watched a movie in the living room, my grandmother took a handful of sleeping pills, closed the door to the bedroom she shared with my little brother, and attempted to take her life by grasping a leather cord in both hands and pulling it tight around her neck. When my mother came home from her holiday party, she heard a rasping noise as she approached the bedroom. I stood behind Esther when she opened the door. Grandma was lying on the bed, her muscular arms raised by her head. The cord was black, knotted on both ends. Esther freed Grandma, then called an ambulance, saving her life. She lived out the rest of her wretched days in state hospitals.

I would like to say I felt compassion, but all I felt was my own suffocation. I understood that if I let it happen, I'd be stuck forever in the role I'd been assigned: serving the needs of those around me who had not learned to navigate the world on their own power and who never doubted that I was born to do it for them. I doubled my resolve to escape, but I didn't yet know how. As I dreamed, Pirate Jenny's words rang in my ears: "And the ship / The Black Freighter / Disappears out to sea / And / On / It / Is / Me."

I've listened to Simone ever since, always with the same feeling of respect and affirmation. I love so much of her music. I'm also moved by the way she made other artists' work her own, like the 1994 version of Jay Hawkins' "I Put a Spell on You"—which might be my favorite—or Bob Dylan's "I Shall Be Released" on the 1969 album *To Love Somebody.*

I wasn't brought up in a musical household, never learned to play an instrument, and at long last, with great effort, learned in my forties to carry a tune well enough to sing along at a birthday party or in shul. Yet music had been solace from the first, sometimes to the point of obsession. I've been known to acquire twenty different versions of a song that aligns my mind, body, feelings, and spirit, cycling through all twenty until I've driven everyone within earshot mad. I've had a blog for nearly two decades, and always finish each post with a song that adds a dimension to what I have written. And while some people bemoan the loss of interaction as we move through city streets plugged into our phones, I see us as self-medicating with music, choosing playlists titrated to our moods.

Decades after I first encountered Nina Simone, I found myself writing about the uses of art, the centrality of culture to human society, seizing on words the critic Walter Pater had written 150 years earlier. "All art constantly aspires towards the condition of music," Pater said, noting that in music, subject matter and form are indistinguishable. This insight has unlocked so much ordinary wisdom. If I want to strike up a real dialogue with someone hard to reach—say a politician sitting behind a desk who can't be troubled to stop reading the mail while I attempt to engage—I only have to find a way to ask that person to remember a time in youth, lying in the dark, replaying a song that held a powerful secret. Reverie overtakes mundane reality, opening a door to connection.

Is music's place in my life rooted in my first experience of Nina Simone? It must be, because from her I learned that anger and pain can make beauty if they are given their freedom by the one who feels them. I learned that I could count on no one to help me make my way, but I could make it myself. I learned to let music into my body, curl around my heart and brain, bring every cell to consciousness, rock me to sleep and to awareness. I learned to listen with more than my ears.

4

Paul Goodman

*In the Camp of Angels of Freedom, Paul Goodman is the Angel
of the Uncolonized Mind, holding the quality of self-authorization.*

Nineteen sixty-four was a big year for me.
I graduated from high school, planning to
go to art school at Cooper Union in New
York. But I ended up postponing the move
east because not long after graduating, I
married my boyfriend, Lionel, who was in
his final year of journalism studies at San
Francisco State College.

I was seventeen years old. The wedding took place in my family's living room.
A few weeks earlier, my mother had been
called by Lionel's mother, who was over-
whelmed by a family crisis. Lionel's sister,
the same age as I, was pregnant by her
boyfriend. When the news broke, she defended herself by saying Lionel and I were
sleeping together, too. Esther gave me the
choice of marrying or never seeing Lionel
again. Mores changed quickly in those
days. Three years later, Esther took my
brother's high school girlfriend to Planned
Parenthood for birth control. But at my
wedding in 1964, she joked that I should be
wearing black. My best friend, Carla, took
me into the bathroom before the ceremony
to fix my hair. As we stood in front of the

mirror, she urged me to escape with her.
My new husband was blind drunk before
either of us had said "I do." We drove to the
tiny apartment we'd rented in the Haight-
Ashbury and fell into bed. It was the first
time we'd spent an entire night together.

The military draft wouldn't end for
another decade. As the war in Vietnam
began gathering steam, being drafted was
an ever-present threat for young men.
Once he finished college, Lionel lost his
student deferment. Although it was still
early in the Vietnam era, he and his peers
expected to be called up. He consulted a
draft-counseling service sponsored by the
college's Associated Students organization
to help students obtain deferments for their
studies, medical problems, or because they
could not stomach the morality of military
service in Vietnam. Together, we com-
pleted his application for conscientious
objector status. I'd been writing papers for
him and was delighted when they earned
good grades, so I was happy not only to
help but to have a challenging writing
assignment.

I enjoyed my part in the process—there was something of the jailhouse lawyer in it, imagining how one's opponents (the draft board) thought and crafting arguments that would win them over, deciphering Selective Service regulations, looking for loopholes. Lionel's application was approved, and the two young men who ran the draft-counseling service asked if I would like to come work with them. The pay was minimal, but other rewards were rich.

The people I met taught me so much—not only my immediate coworkers but also those I met through the draft resisters' network: Quakers from the Central Committee for Conscientious Objectors; soldiers and sailors who'd gone AWOL and needed advice and a haircut; the angst-ridden young men forced to face the ethical dilemma of the war, knowing that lives, including their own, depended on it.

Decades later, dismissive condemnation of "draft dodgers" became de rigueur, especially if they happened to be running for political office. Of course I met such boys, troubled less by morality than fear or inertia, the ones who drank gallons of water or took psychedelics or overdoses of laxatives right before their induction physicals, hoping to succeed at feigning illness or incapacity. The odds of success were good. Many maladies were listed in the Selective Service regulations as grounds for deferment. We draft counselors had to know them. Even now, they sometimes pop unbidden into my mind. I have no idea what AR57-504 covered, but the number is engraved on my brain. Perhaps it was flat feet, extreme nearsightedness, or Osgood-Schlatter disease, an inflammation below the kneecap that prevented many former football players from being drafted.

The conventional view is that those who escaped the draft did so on account of privilege. Many did. If your father's golf partner served on the local draft board, or if your parents could afford to extend your university studies indefinitely, you could be spared by your social advantage. But in San Francisco, my fellow draft counselors were men and women, Black, white, Asian, Latino, gay and straight, rich and poor, and so were the young men we counseled.

I would never endorse a revival of the military draft. But I sometimes wonder whether our wasteful and wicked military interventions since the sixties would have gone forward with so little public awareness or restraint if every eighteen-year-old had been forced to face the agonies of conscience I saw in the young men I counseled, especially those who wound up in prison for refusing induction or deserting when they could no longer bear the guilt of what they had once understood as their patriotic duty.

The Draft Help office wasn't the only such service on campus. There was a print shop in the next Quonset hut that produced flyers and documents for groups like ours; a dozen like-minded organizations were based in other huts. These student fees–financed activities continued to occupy rows of damp and chilly huts on the quad until two key groups housed there, the Black Students Union and the Third World Liberation Front, staged months of student strikes beginning in late 1968, demanding ethnic studies programs and other educational reforms.

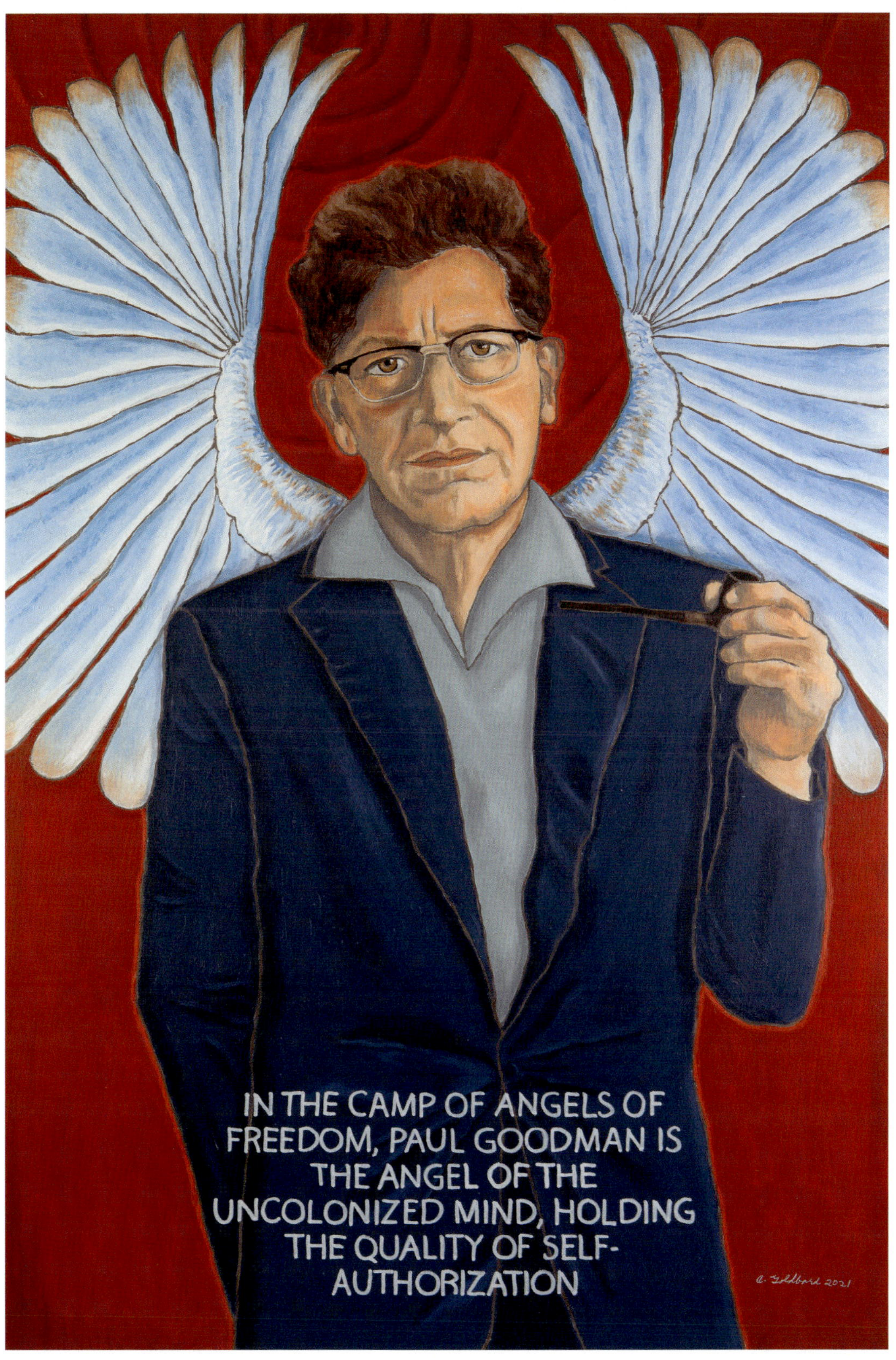
IN THE CAMP OF ANGELS OF
FREEDOM, PAUL GOODMAN IS
THE ANGEL OF THE
UNCOLONIZED MIND, HOLDING
THE QUALITY OF SELF-
AUTHORIZATION

Right next door to our office was the Experimental College, one of the free university experiments that grew up on American campuses in the mid-sixties, when students, frustrated with the limitations of formal curriculum, created their own alternatives. The idea was to offer classes directly relevant to student interests: One class designed a model Black Studies program; another studied the history of peace movements; others focused on the body and movement, psychology, avant-garde art.

The Experimental College had funds to invite a scholar in residence: Paul Goodman, arguably the best-known American intellectual of that time, who wrote and spoke dauntlessly about every subject that engaged him, from Gestalt therapy to city planning to education. I had by then read just one of his books, *Drawing the Line: A Pamphlet,* a collection of political essays published in 1962. The essay my draft-counseling colleagues insisted I read was the first section, "The May Pamphlet," originally published in 1945. Goodman understood himself as an anarchist, a populist, and a libertarian—these terms have acquired different meanings in our day—which to him added up to living as a free being, obliged to call out and oppose authoritarian structures; indeed, to denounce any brake on liberty.

A sentence from that first essay has been inscribed on my heart from the moment I read it: "Free action is to live in present society as though it were a natural society."

There was a sixties word for this: *prefiguration.* I still use it all the time because, to me, it encodes a fundamental principle:

To the extent it is humanly possible, we must treat one another as we would hope to be treated in the loving, equitable, and just society we are working to bring about.

I wish this were practiced more. I am a person of the Left, but I cannot deny that some progressive organizations fall as far short of this standard as their counterparts on the Right. On the small scale, some exploit the society's existing systems, making whatever promises are required to extract resources to support their work from corporations and the like while postponing radical change until the revolution—however it is conceived—is fulfilled. Working conditions are sometimes worse than those they protest. On the global scale, we see the same approach operating in some nations that, having freed themselves from an authoritarian or colonial power, impose a system that suppresses free expression and perpetuates inequality, offering a different rationale for essentially the same choices their oppressors made. If your mission, like Goodman's, is calling out hypocrisy, you can be assured of steady work.

Goodman was invited to San Francisco State in part because his most popular book, the 1960 volume *Growing Up Absurd: Problems of Youth in the Organized System,* focused on a powerful critique of the sort of banking education (to borrow a term from Paulo Freire, another of my angels, who compared conventional schooling to depositing coins in a bank) that was even then dominant. Goodman had a lively time on campus, always eager to talk, full of opinions, thrilled to encounter so many young people who wanted to learn and engage.

He also regularly made himself obnoxious by his relentless pursuit of the young men hanging around the Experimental College. Goodman was a long-married family man with a beloved wife and children, and a powerful drive toward bisexuality. In earlier days, he had repeatedly lost jobs due to what his employers—the University of Chicago, *Partisan Review,* and others—condemned as sexual transgressions. In sixties San Francisco, he evidently hoped the sexual revolution would open space for his desires to be not only expressed but fulfilled, as they sometimes were. He wasn't ostracized, but in his mid-fifties, I think he often seemed merely old and annoying to many of the teenagers and young men he pursued. It was the first time I understood that someone might be brilliant and groundbreaking but also irksome, and neither canceled the other.

Goodman's greatest influence on my own life and work turned on the freedom he felt to comment on any subject that caught his interest. Increasingly since his day, the bias toward credentialed expertise over lived wisdom has distorted our society. Goodman graduated from New York public schools and City College, then pursued higher education in a drawn-out, desultory fashion. But his lack of prestigious diplomas never stopped him from exercising his right to speak, to publish novels, plays, and nonfiction books, to write countless essays and letters to the editor, reminding public figures of their duty to liberty and justice—in other words, to use his mind and voice as he wished. To me, he became the embodiment of the uncolonized mind, one truly free of cant and ideology, always questioning, imagining, and discovering without barriers.

Goodman epitomized the right to be self-authorizing as a citizen of a society or of the world. The desire to see this right extended and multiplied has been a driving force in my work. I hate the extent to which people who lack formal credentials have been silenced by those with the social and economic power that breeds entitlement.

Goodman's explanation for this has inspired my own chutzpah. His response to the criticism that being a polymath might also mean he spread himself too thin and lacked respect for knowledge specialties was simple. Goodman said he had only one subject, "the human beings I know in their man-made scene." He thought that seeing people as whole subjects created more possibility—more grounds for optimism—than peering at them through the lens of one discipline. I agree.

A 1962 essay collection, *The Society I Live in Is Mine,* includes a great many letters to the editor in which he writes of various august bodies and personages, commenting on their transgressions against liberty and justice: the head of the Federal Communications Commission, President Kennedy, the New York Board of Education, every major newspaper, and too many others to list.

For me, the book's title says it all. The word *citizen* has fallen out of favor in some circles because of its association with border walls and official papers, because it has been used as a club to beat immigrants. But a core concept in my own work is the idea of "cultural citizenship," which requires no passport. It describes the right of all to be at home in our own communities, to be met by our neighbors with curiosity and friendliness, to be acknowledged for our contributions to history and society. In a condition of full cultural citizenship, everyone belongs and no one has the right to deny it.

The concept of belonging has been gaining currency for the last decade or so. Much of my work has been in the realm of cultural policy, the aggregate of values, customs, rules, and regulations governing the public interest in culture. Here in the United States, the conventional approach to the subject is pretty much the province of academics and their institutions. Their primary engagement is with a small subset of possible cultural interventions, things like grants to artists and arts organizations, which matter but don't go to the heart of the question: How can society manifest inclusive, democratic cultural values and aims, supporting all people in fulfilling their capabilities? Inspired by Goodman's encompassing sense of social responsibility, one of my desires has been to help expand this understanding beyond the limits imposed by credentialed knowledge. Realizing that this energy had to come from outside the institutional structures that defend the status quo launched me on a lifelong self-directed study of cultural policy. I doubt

my ideas will topple the status quo, but, like Goodman, I believe that putting them into circulation is a precondition for any positive change.

Here's one example: A few years ago I designed a policy on belonging, rooted in the right to culture asserted in the UN's Universal Declaration of Human Rights. It can be adopted by anyone, really—an institution, voluntary association, government—willing to vet proposed actions for their impact on belonging before they are rejected, modified, or adopted. Following such a policy, a school district couldn't drop bilingual classes that were serving students, for instance; a planning department couldn't level a long-standing neighborhood to erect a new sports stadium, obliterating painstakingly cocreated culture; transgender students couldn't be expelled for dressing to express their identity.

This type of citizenship should itself be self-evident and self-authorizing. I would like to believe anyone can have some impact in making it so. But for me, who had been slotted into so many maligned categories—Jew, immigrant, autodidact, working-class, to name a few—and so often encouraged to know and keep my place, it was authorized by Paul Goodman's shining example. I will never stop being grateful.

5

Doris Lessing

*In the Camp of Angels of Freedom, Doris Lessing is the
Angel of Fractured Wholeness, holding the quality of inquiry.*

My first marriage was a soap opera. At seventeen, in 1964, I was far too young to distinguish love from lust, let alone infatuation. When my mother delivered her ultimatum—marry or end the relationship—I felt I couldn't live without the man who became my husband. Once Lionel and I were married, it came instantly clear that all those beers and bourbons at college parties were the daily fare of an alcoholic. I spent many nights sitting at the window of our tiny apartment, peering at the street below for Lionel to stagger home after the bars closed.

I told no one, lest the disapproval of friends or family would worsen the shame and regret I felt for having made such a marriage, for the life it landed me. When we visited Lionel's family, his mother— who reminded me of a small darting bird, sharp and abrupt—told me it had been a challenge to adjust to having someone of a different race in the family: a Jew. I had a tedious job selling gloves and hosiery at a department store. The store had been a San Francisco institution, tasteful,

swanky yet slightly austere. Within a decade it had closed, as the sixties made so many of its mainstays obsolete: hats, gloves, stockings, corsets. Many loyal customers seemed ancient, and probably were. If I close my eyes now, I have a sense memory of trying gloves on the hands of prospective customers. I knew it wasn't nice to think so, but smoothing the thin leather or cotton over their swollen fingers felt like handling a water balloon.

The other saleswomen showed me something of women's common predicament. One wept in the little space we used for lunch and coffee breaks because her husband expected her to mop the kitchen floor every night after supper. She wanted to know if his demand was normal. The other clerks agreed it was excessive. It sounded so to me, too, but mostly it made me wonder what the rules of housecleaning were, as I had never heard them. When I was growing up, my family's idea of tidying was to gesture toward straightening the toppling piles of paper and half-eaten bags of cookies that had rendered the kitchen table obsolete, or the grocery bags stuffed with mail that tumbled onto my feet each time I opened the hall closet. I had considered it real progress that I hadn't started a trash collection of my own.

From time to time, in a reflective mood, one of the women would make a declaration about her purpose in life. It was almost always that her fulfillment arose from making a man happy. This was understood to entail cooking, cleaning, ironing, and more. One night, Lionel and I had dinner with another couple. The husband was a junior reporter at the same paper where Lionel worked, the wife another very young bride. I tried out the statement of purpose I'd heard at work; the bride nodded along. It was just a flash, but I thought I saw the men smirk before wiping their faces clean of expression. To hear us say aloud what they evidently hoped was true, that our value lay in serving them—later I wondered if it had just sounded too good to be true.

For the first year or so of marriage, that was my life. I worked until five, took the bus home, then shopped along Haight Street for the meals I would make, cooking having become a great solace, as it still is for me.

Carla, my best friend from high school, had also moved to San Francisco to attend the same college where I went to work as a draft counselor. She brought me news of her classes and relationships and we talked about the political ferment brewing on campus. She also brought me a novel, one it seemed everyone was reading: Doris Lessing's *The Golden Notebook,* published in 1962. When I think of that book, I see myself sitting on the couch in our tiny Haight-Ashbury apartment with its cheap Indian cotton bedspreads for curtains and hand-me-down furniture, glancing at the clock to see if I had time for one more chapter before starting dinner.

The book is an account of the fragmentation of British society, a prismatic view told through interspersed excerpts from four different color-coded notebooks and a narrative of the main characters' lives. It is a novel of ideas, but the ideas are transmitted through descriptions of ordinary interactions. It would be many months before I became aware of the women's movement or heard the phrase "the personal is political." But Lessing made that point without slogans. What is felt by the women she wrote about had just as much to show the reader as what they think and do. Even though the particulars of age and place were very different from my own world, the narrative sections entitled "Free Women" seemed transcribed from life. Not mine, but the life I might have been living if not for my precipitous marriage. The life I imagined as I chopped vegetables and stirred them into soup.

Nearly sixty years later, whole sections of the book float uninvited onto my mind screen. "I sat and luxuriated in my body. Even a small dry wrinkling of skin on the inside of my thigh, the beginning of being old, gave me pleasure." The voice is Anna Wulf's, the book's main character. I'd been taught to glance past the aspects of reality I feared or disliked, to focus on what might be distracting or pleasant or simply expected. But Lessing wrote with complete willingness to face reality in all of its contradictions and complexity. The message I

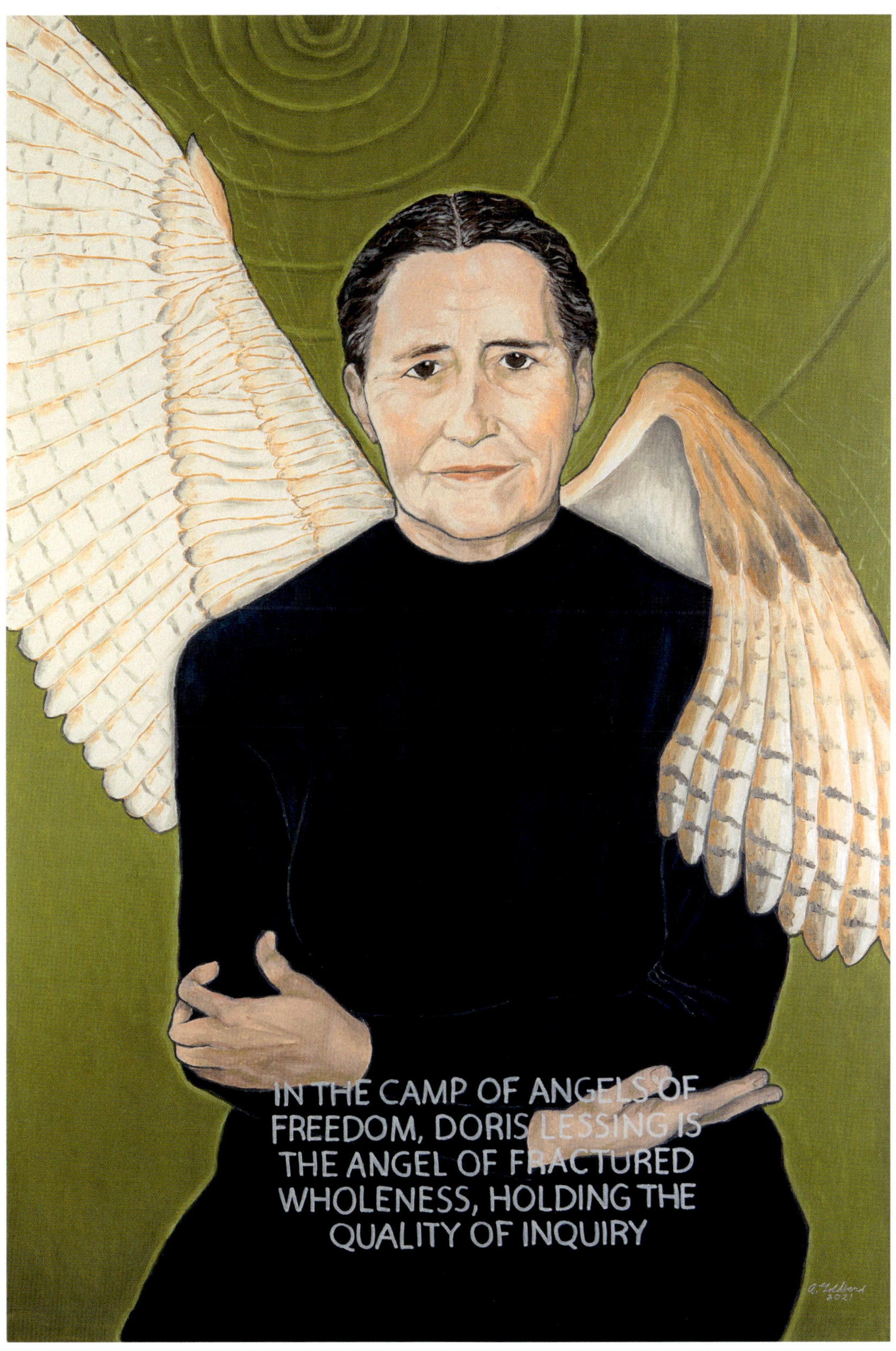

IN THE CAMP OF ANGELS OF
FREEDOM, DORIS LESSING IS
THE ANGEL OF FRACTURED
WHOLENESS, HOLDING THE
QUALITY OF INQUIRY

took from this intricate book was simple: Don't look away. All of it matters.

Even then, still a teenager, I was some type of political animal. The draft counseling, the antiwar demonstrations, the counterculture growing up around me—all of these told young people that our ideas about society truly mattered, that we were obliged to nurture and, as far as we could, enact them. All social arrangements and values must be scrutinized. But the expectations that circumscribed women's roles didn't enter my awareness as quickly or sharply as ideas about war or capitalism or race. I can pinpoint when they did, though, all of a sudden, like a camera clicking into focus.

Carla brought me a pamphlet called "I Want a Wife." It became a classic after being published in the preview issue of *Ms.* magazine in 1971, but this was earlier. The author, Judy Syfers (later returning to her maiden name, Judy Brady)—a wife and mother herself—realized that she, too, would like to have a wife, understood as the person who takes care of every need, uncomplainingly supporting her spouse through school; doing the shopping, cooking, serving, cleaning, and tending to well-behaved children; cultivating and arranging all aspects of social life; being sexually compliant and undemanding; and so on. The first thing I stopped doing was ironing Lionel's shirts. Many other refusals followed. *The Golden Notebook* was not a programmatic book, written to support a feminist political agenda, but by portraying women in command of their own lives, it ignited a sense of the possible.

Lessing helped me discover that opening one's eyes to one aspect of life quickly led to other awakenings, chiefly about the political milieu I inhabited. From *The Golden Notebook,* I learned how easily people live inside a political culture that commands them to look away, something I was to experience often.

Lessing was involved in the Communist Party, and, like many in her generation, was finally disillusioned by the truths of Stalinist repression revealed after the 20th Party Congress in Moscow in 1956. She was extremely good at depicting British Party members rehearsing the orthodoxies and groupthink that supplant inquiry in a controlling culture. I was impressed by her portrayal of the desperate desire for a figure of the good father who understands, who cares. In one passage, Anna Wulf recounts a Party member's story submitted for publication. Comrade Ted, chosen for a delegation to the Soviet Union, comes upon kindly Comrade Stalin working late at an ordinary desk. Ted is flattered to be asked for his opinion on Party policy in Great Britain, delivers a three-hour monologue that mesmerizes Stalin, and returns home uplifted and refreshed. The committee members who vet the manuscript fall into uncomfortable laughter, remembering how often they'd seen essentially the same fantasy recounted: Stalin consults one protagonist on European policy, tells a pair of workers how to fix their tractor, etc.

I can't count how many times this scene has come to mind since I first read the book, only the good father I've heard people fantasize about has been Reagan, Obama, or Trump.

After *The Golden Notebook*, I read every Lessing novel as soon as I could get my hands on it. I loved them all. Some readers disliked the "space fiction" series—*Shikasta* and its sequels. Reporting on planet Earth from the perspective of emissaries of an advanced alien civilization, those books were influenced by Lessing's study of Sufism. They enthralled me. I loved lifting the veil of conventional vision to see our own world in a completely new way, through the eyes of narrators who considered it not the center of the universe nor the apex of civilization, but just another place that needed help.

Lessing's easy way with the absurd failure of society showed me the arbitrariness of customs and expectations. Through her writing, I understood that I was in charge of my own education, that as I began to know myself, what I had to offer and what I wanted, it became increasingly clear that there would be no mentor or institution to guide me.

I was helped by the emergent ethos of the counterculture. In those days, a do-it-yourself attitude permeated every aspect of living: People not only made their own bread; they ground the flour. I sat through hundreds of meetings, almost always with a piece of fabric, thread, and scissors on my lap. I managed to embroider some sort of decoration on nearly every article of clothing we owned, most of which were homemade or rescued from the thrift shop. If we needed a plant holder—I can't recall why plants had to cascade from the ceiling instead of sitting quietly on saucers, but they did—I would macramé it. If I needed an envelope, a far more common occurrence than in the age of email, I would fold and glue a piece of rice paper into the requisite shape.

Underpinning this DIY orientation was a sweeping critique of the dominant culture and its conventions. We had to do it ourselves because the conventionally done thing was so paltry and trifling. Institutions were stultifying, shaped by pointless rules and bureaucratic excess. Social conventions were idiotic, boxing people into lives they hated, prizing decorum over truth and responsibility.

Not being a student, I wasn't involved in campus activism per se, but I was an enthusiastic participant in 1967's Vietnam Summer organizing, the Spring Mobilization to End the War in Vietnam, and the mass actions that followed, serving on committees, designing flyers, marching in the streets. To myself and my friends, it appeared that our way of looking at society was in the ascendancy, that it was only a matter of time before oppressive social institutions gave way to new forms of relationship more loving, reciprocal, democratic, and just.

We were wrong, of course, which became clear the minute Ronald Reagan was elected president in 1980. I might have seen it sooner if I had read Lessing's political novels—*The Good Terrorist, The Memoirs of a Survivor, The Four-Gated City,* and the Canopus in Argos novels—as warnings rather than imaginative stories. Today, it is clear that the greatest changes catalyzed by the sixties have been aspects of personal liberty and behavior. My young self would have been delighted to know that marijuana and same-sex marriage would become legalized, to be sure, that organic food, alternative medicine, and solar energy were to become commonplace. But it is crushing to accept that the polarization of wealth has greatly worsened, that corporate domination has only increased, that racism and anti-Semitism have flourished, that women are still not safe on their own streets or in their own homes and offices, that life on Earth is at extreme risk.

Perhaps twenty years ago, a friend who dabbled in psychic practice told me that I had come here from another planet where wicked problems like inequality and racism had been solved, which accounted for my perpetually can-do attitude here on Earth. I like this very much as a metaphor, if not a literal account. Perhaps it explains my affinity for speculative fiction, but a straight line also connects this propensity with Less-

ing, with immersing myself in *The Golden Notebook* all those years ago. I have a shelf of unpublished fiction manuscripts in my office, and almost every one, as with the two novels I have published, turns on some type of supernatural event or extrasensory perception.

From Doris Lessing I learned to ignore the fences the dominant society erects around the forms of information a stratified, capitalistic, quantification-addicted society prizes. She taught me to see through conventional ways of reading the world to a much richer story woven from body, emotion, intellect, and spirit. I learned to insist that all these forms of information matter greatly, and that we look away at our peril.

6

Alice Neel

In the Camp of Angels of Freedom, Alice Neel is the Angel of Impassioned Persistence, holding the quality of dauntlessness.

Once I started painting, I never imagined I would stop. But I did stop, sometimes for long periods, and almost always because work for social justice called me. Each time I resumed, more than anything else, it was Alice Neel's vivid, penetrating, fearless portraits that brought me back.

In the sixties, I was called to take part in draft counseling and antiwar organizing. I did a great many posters and flyers for movement organizations and events. I had a dream that a painting I made had stopped the war in Vietnam, but when I woke up and went to my easel, I couldn't remember what it looked like.

My first marriage ended around the time of that dream. I was twenty-two and desperately unhappy. I no longer waited at the window until the bars closed, but neither did I expect to see Lionel walk through the door at the end of the day. I read more deeply into the powerful and persuasive writings of the rising women's movement. That set me to question much more than the compliant way I'd cooked, cleaned, ironed, and deferred. The default institutions I'd always accepted as somehow inevitable no longer made sense: marriage, family, money, power. In the time of dislocation that followed, I did not paint.

I had two close friends who understood my situation. George, with whom I'd gone to school, and Anya, a much older woman who'd met George when they both studied music with the same teacher, and who had become his lover. That choice ended her ice-cold marriage to the unpleasant man her own age who'd ensconced her in a penthouse, the kind that had a direct elevator and a basket of slippers by the door to protect the highly polished floors from visitors' shoes. The kind I'd seen only in a movie.

We three became inseparable. I think it was because—despite all the outward incongruities—we accepted one another absolutely. Anya had been born in Russia to an adored father, a gambler and adventurer she described as shrewd and combative, and a mother she never mentioned. Anya had been a dancer in the corps de ballet of the Ballet Russe de Monte Carlo. She liked to reminisce about her role as one of the four cygnets in *Swan Lake*. She wore her sandy hair tightly pulled back, topped by a large braided chignon that emphasized the sharp angle of her long nose, her hooded eyes under false lashes. Her fingernails were long and thickly painted an icy beige. She wore cashmere sweaters and a heavy gold ring set with a carved aquamarine. George was a large man, towering over Anya, but delicate in his movements. By day, he delivered mail for the post office, which seemed a comedown, given his prior aspirations as a musician. None of us fit anywhere, but life had taken us to unexpected destinations, and that brought us together.

On the last night of my first marriage, Lionel and I had a date to see the Truffaut film *Jules et Jim* with George and Anya. The three of us waited at home for my husband, finally deciding to leave without him rather than miss the film. Excepting her beauty, there was little to admire in Catherine, the character Jeanne Moreau played with elemental force. But she was such an embodiment of willful self-determination that watching her gave me the courage to leave the marriage.

Alice Neel would never have been mistaken for Jeanne Moreau, but when I first encountered Neel and her work, she had that same impact, pure will in a woman's body.

I set about discovering the life of a single woman, a new experience, as I'd skipped straight from high school into married life. George gave me a place to live, a place to set up my easel, too. On the living room wall, I hung a large painting of a man I knew. Neel's fearless nude portraits had inspired me. The reclining figure slept on a couch,

arms crossed under his beard, naked from the waist down. A couple of neighbors worked for a thriving hard-core movie business. Glancing in the window as they passed and seeing the picture gave them the idea of renting the place for a shoot. For a week or two, when I came home at the end of the day, the apartment was filled with sweaty people wrapped in towels, tidying up.

I became friends with another young woman who had taken part in a draft-counseling course my colleagues and I had offered. She'd come to California from the East Coast, following her on-and-off partner, who manufactured a special brand of LSD. He sold it wholesale, to dealers. Each set of tiny translucent squares came in a cunning wooden box designed by a local artisan, wrapped with a length of hand-woven ribbon.

This was new. The counterculture may have looked unitary from the outside, but it had two camps. Lionel and I had situated ourselves on the political side, not that of the drug culture. We had smoked a little dope, but that's all. Our first experience was with some of his college classmates in a tiny cupola on the top story of an old Victorian in a run-down part of San Francisco. All the walls had been covered in tinfoil. People kept asking the same question: *Do you feel anything yet?* Now I dropped acid with my new friend on the beach north of San Francisco. We fell asleep on deserted sand and woke up, full-on tripping, surrounded by tourists and dogs, deeply sunburned on one side of our faces and bodies.

In 1969, I went to the Rolling Stones concert at the Altamont Speedway in the East Bay. This was supposed to be the West

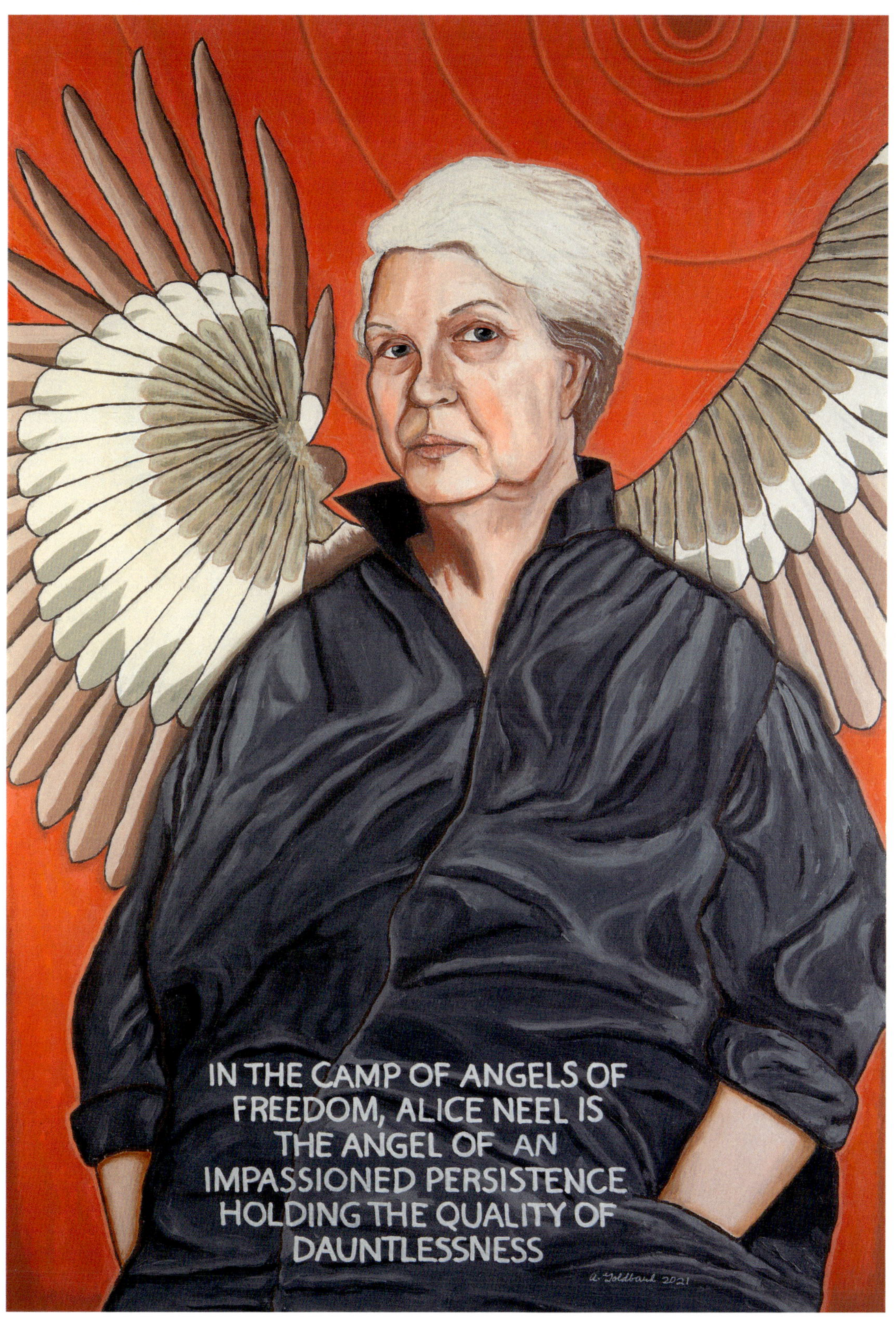

IN THE CAMP OF ANGELS OF
FREEDOM, ALICE NEEL IS
THE ANGEL OF AN
IMPASSIONED PERSISTENCE
HOLDING THE QUALITY OF
DAUNTLESSNESS

Coast response to Woodstock, which had taken place a few months earlier. Santana was going to play, the Jefferson Airplane, even the Grateful Dead. The hot, dry racetrack was crowded and scary, amphetamines and alcohol setting the tone rather than the ego-dissolving psychedelics that first fueled the sixties. The concert is remembered for the violence it engendered, the Stones having engaged the Hells Angels motorcycle gang to provide security. This phenomenally stupid decision led to injury and death, including the beating and stabbing of eighteen-year-old Meredith Hunter, who, driven from the stage by the Angels, returned holding a gun and was killed.

Counterculture activism continued for a long time—in my circles, it was commonplace to say the sixties lasted into the late seventies—but peace and love were giving way to power, for better and worse. People were going their separate ways. The Black Panther Party became the vanguard of Black liberation through both social programs—free breakfasts for kids, community health clinics, and more—and a philosophy of self-defense that advocated repaying the violence of white supremacy with armed insurrection. The multiracial civil rights movement morphed into a movement of self-determination for Black Power. The FBI responded with covert action through COINTELPRO, assassinating Black Panther Party leader Fred Hampton just two days before Meredith Hunter, also Black, was killed at Altamont.

The little world of private life faded, replaced by collectivity. If I made art, it was to illustrate an antiwar poster; if it couldn't serve something larger, it wasn't worth doing. Even in relatively benign realms such as draft counseling, politics became more serious, doctrinaire, and potentially dangerous for everyone involved. Still, we thought our actions were repairing the world. We thought the right response was to redouble them.

In 1970, I was contacted by a former classmate of Lionel's whom I'd helped apply for conscientious objector status. He had moved to Portland to work on an underground newspaper. He invited me to visit. That led to my moving north for several years, living in collectives and working on the paper. Each week we were given a pile of papers to sell on street corners in lieu of salary. Life was one long meeting, some productive but many merely enactments of interpersonal political drama inspired by revolution in the developing world.

For instance, most people in the collectives I knew became acquainted with "criticism/self-criticism" ("crit/self-crit" for short) by reading *Fanshen,* a 1966 book by William Hinton that laid out Chinese Communist Party strategy for building a rural power base. Those who liked the practice described it as a humble and effective way for people to improve by confessing their own misdeeds and misunderstandings and helping others to do likewise. But from what I could see, those who liked it most enjoyed abusing others through coerced confessions to minor sins—*You shaved your legs! You left the dishes!*—performing rituals of public humiliation that showed everyone precisely where authority lay, no matter what was said about sharing power. The women's movement had taught us that the personal is political, but not always in a good way.

Living in a collective was confusing. I couldn't fall back on convention. I made many dumb mistakes, such as walking into a room without knocking because knocking suddenly seemed obsolete. I was filled with regret at the shocked faces of the half-dressed occupants, who stumbled over their words because they couldn't bring themselves to say something as bourgeois as "Please knock." I left a valued keepsake in a drawer in our bedroom and came home to find it gone. I was stymied into silence at the mere thought of an accusation; how could I protest if property itself was understood to be theft? I wonder now if the rude awakenings of the period were simply a kind of slam dance: deluding ourselves that the world we desired was already here, then repeatedly being jolted out of that self-induced trance, each jolt a reminder of how wrong we were.

I learned a lot working on the paper, though, chiefly layout and editing skills. When the IRS decimated the underground newspaper movement by charging these ramshackle and impoverished groups with violations of the tax code, we moved back to the Bay Area. I looked for graphic design work, finding a job at the San Francisco Neighborhood Arts Program, an early experiment in community-based arts. I designed flyers and printed them on a mimeograph machine.

I started painting again for the first time since my marriage to Lionel had ended. I once again experienced the freedom Alice Neel described, once again wondered how I could ever have let it go: "The minute I sat in front of a canvas I was happy," Neel said, "because it was a world, and I could do what I liked in it."

This time was a turning point for me. Poets and painters, dancers and actors would come by the office to commission flyers. I entered a world of quirk and color and possibility.

Through these networks of artists and activists, I began to understand something about the social structures and economies that sustained cultural work. I saw that the same inequities that marred every other social sector distorted the cultural sector. Important decisions (often funded by taxpayers) affected everyone but were controlled by a few powerful people who also felt entitled to proclaim aesthetic value, asserting a dominant standard that mostly excluded women and artists of color. I began speaking out. I read about protests by artists in New York against museums' racial bias. I saw photos of Alice Neel on the picket line at the Museum of Modern Art and the Whitney. Not long after, I became lead organizer for a group called the San Francisco Art Workers' Coalition.

I left my partner and eventually moved into my own apartment in San Francisco. I did my best to teach myself graphic design and production. If I didn't know how to do something, I said I did and found a library book. I began to get freelance jobs as an illustrator and graphic designer.

Those were my day jobs. I set up a studio in my spare bedroom and painted portraits—pictures based on old photographs, self-portraits, pictures of anyone I could persuade to sit for me. All I have now are photographs of the panels I had asked my mother to store. In the images I have left, I see a clear through line: Some were scaled to include the whole body, others just head and shoulders, but all recorded head-on, eyes-open encounters with a palpable presence.

I was always drawn to portraiture as my art form. That has never changed. The human subject interests me because it seems to contain all there is: what is feared and desired, the marks left by the years, the marks that cannot be seen but somehow emerge from long contemplation.

In the early seventies, some of my sitters were strangers. One was the roommate of a friend, another a young woman who'd recently moved to town and surely consented to sit out of loneliness. On first meeting, I remember feeling I didn't much like her. But that didn't matter. Sittings were transformative. Stationing myself close enough to breathe the same air, staring at someone's face and body, chatting about something urgent or nothing much, the boundaries between my sitter and myself softened. Something rushed in; I have to call it love. I understood that to encounter another human being without preconception, to allow time and space to reveal that person's presence, to be open to receiving whatever emerged created a connection free of judgment, an unimpeded flow.

"I do not pose my sitters," Neel once said. "I do not deliberate and then concoct. . . . Before painting, when I talk to the person, they unconsciously assume their most characteristic pose, which in a way involves all their character and social standing—

what the world has done to them and their retaliation."

The way Neel talked about her work gave me permission to be self-authorizing as a visual artist, as Paul Goodman had granted me permission with respect to thought and speech. I had very little knowledge of art-world orthodoxies and customs or about accepted or conventional approaches to painting. I had no way to understand or situate myself in the stream of artmaking and art exhibition. Everything I knew, I learned by doing.

From the first time I encountered her, the advice I could extract from reading an interview with Neel or seeing her paintings in an art journal felt like a thrillingly reliable guide to my own choices. I knew she had to struggle greatly to continue making work, that she resented not getting her due and reveled when it finally arrived. I knew she held her ground as a portraitist despite the ascendancy of Abstract Expressionism. I knew that I would have to do the same despite the ascendancy of installation art, despite a pervasive feeling that painting was dead except for what was admiringly called "bad painting," despite the fact that my own painting lacked the visual tropes that characterized the work emerging from art schools. That was just a different way to be other, something I'd become used to long ago.

When I stopped painting for a few years later in the seventies, it was during a long period devoted to organizing intended to awaken fellow artists to the potential power of solidarity, especially around issues like public funding and other aspects of cultural policy. I came to a place where what I accepted as political truth too powerfully contradicted the accepted truths of artmaking. In my talks and writings, I had compared artists to Sleeping Beauty, passively waiting for the prince—the gallerist, funder, patron—to deliver the kiss of life. How could I enact that same tired drama in my own life? In the political worlds I inhabited, easel painting was considered trivial, making objects to decorate the walls of the privileged, and artists were people who, if they were lucky, got paid for playing. How could I place myself in that frame? I began to regard myself much more as an organizer than as a visual artist. I fell into the trap of seeing myself as people had looked at one another in the crit/self-crit circle: ripe for correction, politically negligible, too involved with my own feelings.

My organizing work moved into speaking, writing, and consulting. I went to Sacramento to set up a technical assistance service for artists at the California Arts Council during the first term of Governor Jerry Brown. There I met my second husband, Dave. We didn't last long in Sacramento, as the governor's enemies used Brown's fondness for the Arts Council against him, scrutinizing the agency for even the most minor departure from bureaucratic practice, making our lives a misery of surveillance. We wrote damning resignation letters and left.

After a few years in San Francisco, we moved to a small town two hours north and I resumed painting with a series of portraits that used the globe as a metaphor. In my self-portrait, I stand wrapped in an apron, wooden spoon in hand, cradling a swaddled bundle on one hip. Where the head of an infant would be, I painted a small image of the Earth.

Then I stopped painting for the longest time. From the mid-eighties on, I did the odd drawing, and I designed and illustrated publications I'd written. But I didn't begin painting again until 2019 in New Mexico, where I now live, when my life came to a turning. I'd devoted myself for years to a few organizing projects, but I was no longer learning from them. All that was keeping me in the work was other people feeling I was needed. A wise person asked me what I had done that gave me joy and pleasure. I replied that having been rained out on vacation earlier that year, I had turned to drawing and loved it. I was advised to keep drawing without a goal, to see what emerged. That led to a return to the studio, a portrait of my third and much-loved husband, Rick, and, since then, perhaps a dozen portraits before I embarked on "In the Camp of Angels of Freedom," pushed by the pandemic to abandon painting from life.

Each time I returned to painting, I gained a deeper understanding of art as the practice of freedom. Each time, painting welcomed me as a refugee from some imposed idea of meaning, purpose, and value. Each time, I saw Alice Neel as the embodiment of this truth.

There are videos on the internet of Neel in her later years giving talks or being interviewed by critics and curators. She plays off the grandmotherly softness of her appearance, making sly or self-deprecating comments that elicit laughs from the audience. But how could someone who'd lived Neel's life have been soft? A lost child, time in a mental hospital after a suicide attempt, a long stretch raising sons on public assistance in a Spanish Harlem walk-up, and much more. I could see the steel beneath the softness and tried to show it in her portrait. I thought she deserved that.

I've bought several Alice Neel books in the last few years, and also spent a great deal of time clicking around websites featuring her work. I knew she would guide me. I love that her own story had a happy ending—the honors and acknowledgments denied her earlier all came through in the last part of her life—but that had nothing to do with it. I don't see my own story heading that way. From Alice Neel, I learned to find my place among those who know what kind of instruments they are, know the music that is theirs to play, and, despite setbacks, refuse to abandon this truth. "You should keep on painting no matter how difficult it is," said Neel, "because this is all part of experience, and the more experience you have, the better it is . . . unless it kills you, and then you know you have gone too far."

7

Paulo Freire

In the Camp of Angels of Freedom, Paulo Freire is the Angel of Critical Consciousness, holding the quality of self-determination.

When I think of Paulo Freire's influence on my life, I see myself in the passenger seat of a down-at-the-heels pumpkin-colored Datsun traveling three hundred miles up the California coast from San Francisco to Arcata. I am reading aloud from Freire's masterwork, *Pedagogy of the Oppressed,* glimpses of redwood trees whizzing by whenever I lift my gaze. Closing my eyes now, I can see the place where the road narrows and we drive through an archway carved into the trunk of a giant sequoia.

The book was heavy going, translated to English from the original Portuguese, with what felt like a stop-off in German. I had to look up a word in the very first sentence: *axiological* (it refers to the study of value). One of Freire's core concepts, *conscientizagao,* necessitated a new English word—*conscientization*—defined as "learning to perceive social, political and economic contradictions, and to take action against the oppressive elements of reality."

This was late in the seventies. The Datsun's driver was my second husband, Dave. We were married at the end of 1978,

not long after we left the employ of the California Arts Council, appalled at the agency's inept politicking, disappointed in our hope that working there would help to enact cultural democracy, our ideal of inclusion and equity.

We'd been invited to our jobs in Sacramento to solve two very different problems. Dave was hired by the white-shoe senior bureaucrat who'd been imported from Washington to run the agency. The theory was that someone who knew and represented old-school arts agencies would help to legitimate this state agency experiment designed by figures like the poet Gary Snyder, who lived so far off the grid that there was a budget item for carrier pigeons should an urgent message need to reach him. Dave knew a lot about administrative systems and financial reports; it was hoped his competence would help to balance the creative leaps that had oversight agencies looking askance.

I'd been invited to set up a semi-independent service funded by the Arts Council to provide small grants and technical assistance to artists and organizations, especially those not deemed "mainstream." My brief was to spread help and resources throughout the state, at least gesturing toward balancing the dominant tendency to reserve the lion's share of public funding for red-carpet arts institutions: symphony orchestras, major museums, opera and ballet companies.

Governor Jerry Brown enjoyed engaging with counterculture types, appointing quite a few of them to the governing body of this agency. Before I was invited to Sacramento, I'd helped to produce a newsletter created by Bay Area artists to cover cultural agencies and policies. When Governor Brown's appointees to the Arts Council demonstrated their absolute lack of familiarity with policymaking by proceeding at a public meeting to divide the agency's grant budget by the number of council members and authorize each to select "pet projects" in that amount for funding, satire seemed the only option.

Somehow none of this discouraged council members from offering me funding and more or less carte blanche to set up "Cultural News and Services," nor deterred me from accepting. But after a year and a half of being thwarted at every turn by control agencies whose leaders took their grievances with the governor out on the arts programs rumored to be his favorites, we left. We moved to San Francisco and formed a consulting partnership to help public agencies and arts organizations plan their work and solve cultural problems. Then we moved in together.

Then we got married, among the first batch of people to do so at City Hall once it reopened after the assassinations of Mayor George Moscone and Supervisor Harvey Milk by another supervisor, Dan White, who got off with a very light sentence by employing "the Twinkie defense" to establish diminished capacity. A few days earlier, we'd been in a stationery story buying wedding announcements when the news of their deaths blasted over the loudspeaker. As we drove home, we saw that someone had sprayed "Guyana A-Go-Go" on the posts that supported freeway overpasses, commenting on the "revolutionary suicide" massacre of nearly a thousand local acolytes of the Reverend Jim Jones, founder of the Peoples Temple and a popular and influential supporter of progressive politicians. He had taken his followers to Guyana to escape his enemies, real and imagined. When a member of Congress visited to assess the situation, Jones ordered his followers to drink Kool-Aid mixed with cyanide, first administering the poison to their children.

The spirit of the times was bizarre. Marrying seemed like something positive to do, even though when we told our friends we'd gotten married, they all asked "Why?"

Our marriage was founded on two things: a shared desire to find a sanctuary from the chaos and rejection of our upbringings, and a shared thirst for ideas that could galvanize change. Now, driving through the old-growth forests, we were on our way north to consult with a group of artists who had come to an impasse in their collective work. We must have stopped for gas or food, but in my memory, the six-hour journey was fueled by that flashing

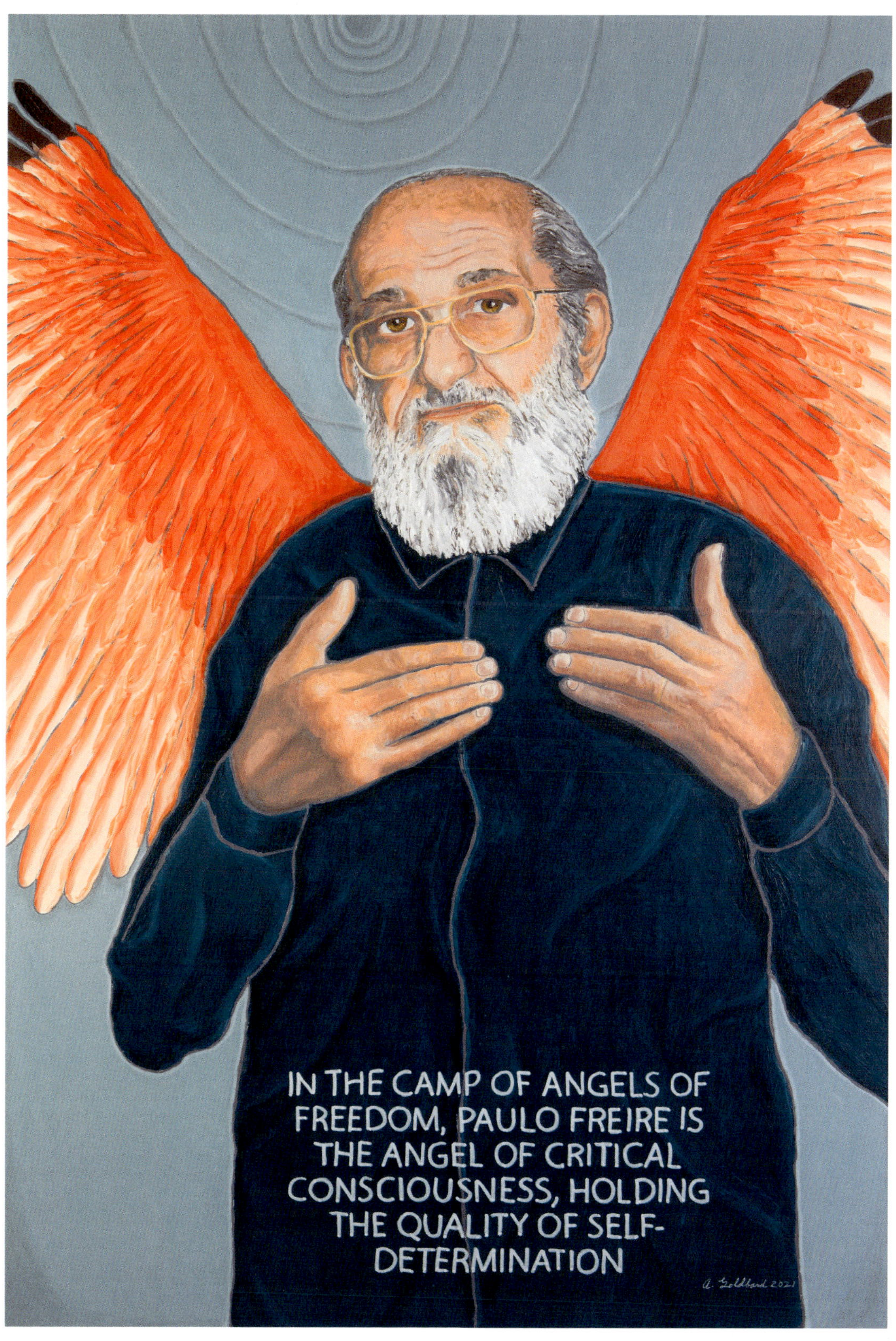

IN THE CAMP OF ANGELS OF
FREEDOM, PAULO FREIRE IS
THE ANGEL OF CRITICAL
CONSCIOUSNESS, HOLDING
THE QUALITY OF SELF-
DETERMINATION

excitement that comes with discovering a new way to look at something familiar. I lived for the pleasure that launches a burst of possibility, lifting a flock of questions into flight. I still do. Reading and discussing Paulo Freire's book one sentence at a time was well worth the effort.

Like most of the organizational conflicts we were privy to early in our consulting practice, this one was presented as a clash of personalities. The group's leader was condemned as too controlling, gossip and whispers abounded, and defensiveness rose in direct proportion to attack. We searched for a way to enlarge the field of inquiry so that what was happening could be understood and acted upon as challenges not for one individual but for the whole organization, not about personalities but about the complexities of connecting culture and community.

Freire came instantly to mind. I had discovered him a few years earlier courtesy of a boyfriend who worked in progressive education: interactive, liberating, egalitarian schools created to nurture the whole person rather than to train test takers. I knew *Pedagogy of the Oppressed* had a great deal to teach me, but I had difficulty comprehending its essence until that journey north, until I had a pressing reason to seek its guidance, until I had a willing partner in the painstaking effort required.

Freire was an educator, whereas our focus was cultural development. We worked with artists and communities who cocreated arts projects—murals, theater, publications, and much more—that expressed values of self-determination, social inclusion, beauty and meaning in the service of

love and justice. But the difference seemed irrelevant. Coming to understand ourselves as building and bearing culture is an educational process, a way of learning by doing and reflecting. As I read each demanding sentence, Freire's essential ideas surged across my brain-heart barrier, instantly changing my way of seeing the world.

In *Pedagogy of the Oppressed,* Freire described a common type of magical thinking in which the processes by which things are accomplished and power accrues are obscure and impenetrable to those without social or economic privilege. Things just happen, as if by magic. He contrasted this with critical consciousness, a stance of questioning that leads first to understanding, then to the power to act, to intervene in the world and help transform it. Freire spoke of "internalization of the oppressor": how the voices of those in power infiltrate the minds of those they dominate; the way they tell us we are stupid, lazy, not good enough, best off leaving important things to those in charge; the ease with which, after infinite repetition, we can mistake their voices for our own and passively comply. I had experienced this many times: allowing myself to be used by family members whose own needs, I was told, always trumped mine; internalizing the idea that "girls don't do" whatever it was that drew me; obeying those who told me that making art was bourgeois triviality.

Freire's liberating pedagogy began with landless peasants in Brazil. The educational challenge first presented to him was overcoming what appeared to the official educational authorities a puzzling resistance to learning to read and write.

It didn't take long to discover the nature of that resistance. First, reading was typically taught through the mindless tropes of primary-school banality; when I was a kid, it was Dick and Jane and "see Spot run." What did such condescension have to do with the lives of these adult learners? Second, the state's sudden interest in agrarian literacy was part of an economic shift from agriculture to manufacturing. You may not need to read to plant and pick crops, but to move to the city for a factory job or a desk job, literacy is essential. Conventional literacy programs were easily understood by those they targeted as part of a strategy for ending their land-based way of life.

Instead of asking how these stubborn people could be made to learn, the question Freire's challenge posed was how literacy could serve the felt needs and actual freedom and well-being of the learners. This was not hard to discern: How could they organize, participate in political processes, press their agenda, and prevent exploitation without the written word?

To engage learners, Freire used what he called "culture circles" to explore "generative themes," meaningful topics that could be discussed in ways that nourished participants' sense of agency. They could be as simple as single words: *culture, work, world.* They were invitations to recognize one's agency in relation to each theme. That led members of a circle to see how the dominant social order disempowered them, and, from there, to understanding they were part of a class with common interests. People thus experienced themselves as subjects in history, as makers of culture, rather than as objects in thrall to those with power.

One of the most compelling aspects of Freire's thinking is his insistence that everyone possesses the same capacities for self-knowledge and self-liberation. His respect for the wisdom emanating from people's own experiences stands in stark contrast to a society in which whole categories of human beings are commonly treated as dispensable, as having nothing to contribute to our collective knowledge and power. Through Freire's work, I determined to reject any system of thought that contradicted the essential equality of human possibility.

On the way to Arcata, Dave and I composed a short story—a fable, really—to serve as a generative theme for the group. Our client fit the category of "entrepreneurial organizations," those experiencing what is sometimes called "founder's syndrome." Such organizations were started by charismatic individuals with bright ideas, those whose charm and vision attracted followers. They typically put their stamp on every aspect of a group's work, so that when its name was mentioned, people would say, "Oh, yes, X's thing."

In our consulting, we'd often seen coworkers fall into conflict when an entrepreneur's charm and vision began to fade and their own need to share power along with their labor began to grow. In this case, the entrepreneurial leader was a young woman absolutely dedicated to her work, but also, as with many such leaders, self-consciously projecting a vivid and unique persona that took up a lot of space. She wanted to be loved and appreciated for her dedication, but also given free rein to put her stamp on the work. Others found it difficult to be heard or heeded if they saw things differently. Our fable was more than the brief word or phrase Freire preferred, but not very complex. It framed the dilemma of an organization—no names—at just such a crossroads. Reading it aloud with the group prepared the ground for a long and revealing conversation in which everyone was given equal speaking and listening space and attention. The group emerged with new working agreements, and we had a new tool to use with troubled organizations.

There has barely been a day in the intervening decades that Freire's wisdom hasn't offered me a key to understanding power dynamics—in organizations, but equally in family patterns, in national and international politics, in the relations of race and gender and sexuality, of social exclusion and inclusion reflected in every cultural manifestation. The context may be an actual family in which grown children endow their father with power such that they constantly seek approval at the cost of suppressing their own gifts and desires. Or it may be vast, the epidemic of magical thinking that persuaded millions of voters to believe that a mendacious millionaire reality-show host could ordain white supremacy forever.

Almost everywhere I look, I see people relinquishing their autonomy and agency to those who've been whispering in their ears, "Surrender; resistance is futile." I see them mistaking those voices for their own, and my heart breaks.

For Freire, the antidote to internalized powerlessness was genuine dialogue. People need to speak openly, listen deeply, to discover their own relationship to the themes being explored through talking together freely, learning from one another. Most of the community-based arts work I know is founded on this same understanding. The dialogue isn't always in words. It might be making music together or devising images for a collective work of visual art. But the same deep truths are always embedded in the process: Liberation emanates from the oppressed, whose knowledge of their own situations surpasses that of all experts, and who, despite all obstacles, when offered the opportunity to deepen and act on that knowledge, will move to free themselves. I know this from my own story, and from those of so many others.

Some of the best moments in my professional life are when I meet people who thank me for my books or talks, saying I have given them language to understand their work as part of something large and powerful. I got to meet Paulo Freire once at a conference. It was near the end of his life, and many people wanted to talk with him, so there was time for just a few words. I thanked him for that gift, which refreshed me, a drink of cool water in the desert.

Freire entered my life in the earliest days of what came to be a bad marriage and a bad business partnership. The joint consulting stopped long before the relationship, though my individual practice continues to this day. When I finally walked out—thirty years later—the realization that propelled me was that I had internalized a voice far more invested in using me than in my well-being. I feel sad when I see that it took me so long to apply Freire's lessons to my own life. I may sometimes be slow on the uptake, but his wisdom has never failed me.

8

Isaiah Berlin

*In the Camp of Angels of Freedom, Isaiah Berlin is the
Angel of Multiplicity, holding the quality of pluralism.*

I can't think of the philosopher and Oxford don Isaiah Berlin without also thinking of a particular speech by Susan Sontag, though as far as I know, they had no personal connection except Sontag's having attended some of Berlin's lectures in the fifties. But there is a connection in my life.

In 1982, Sontag gave a controversial speech at a rally in support of Poland's Solidarity movement. Some previous speakers had expressed their trepidation about being allied in their support for Solidarity with conservative monoliths such as the Reagan administration and the Catholic Church. Sontag said that communism, the "most successful variant of fascism," was "fascism with a human face." She called out the Left for giving Communist regimes a large helping of benefit of the doubt, choosing to see them as allies in opposing the crimes of capitalist states and therefore downplaying their flaws and misdeeds.

She was excoriated by many left-wing intellectuals, some of whom pointed out that communism doesn't need to be called fascism to be indicted for its wrongs; others were appalled by her glowing characterization of right-wing anticommunism: "Imagine, if you will, someone who read only the *Reader's Digest* between 1950 and 1970, and someone in the same period who read only *The Nation* or the *New Statesman*," she had said. "Which reader would have been better informed about the realities of Communism? The answer, I think, should give us pause. Can it be that our enemies were right?"

I learned more from my own reaction than from her speech. At that time, my views defaulted to a far greater suspicion of capitalist states than Communist (now I am an equal-opportunity suspecter). Years before, many of my colleagues had gone to Cuba on Venceremos Brigade trips to harvest sugarcane and receive political education. When I lived in Portland, one of our housemates had been on a similar trip to Cambodia in the time of Pol Pot. She'd come back singing the praises of the Khmer Rouge in language that seemed to be taken directly from a Stalin-era Politburo bulletin. This made me uneasy, but I didn't know what to do with my unease.

I have a vivid memory of hanging out with friends on playground swings in the interstices of a theater conference. One was a veteran of the civil rights movement, the other a professor at a midwestern university. Both men spoke of politics with confidence and certainty. They knew who was and wasn't on the right side of history. During the previous conference session, someone had talked about persecution of sexual minorities in Cuba. Both men condemned that as airing family laundry in public. They insisted that nothing critical could be said about the Soviet Union or other Communist countries because criticizing them would, in effect, be supporting the U.S. government, which was always looking for an excuse to invade, conquer, discredit.

When I pointed out some of the crimes of these regimes—the censorship of art in many countries, the imprisonment of dissidents in China and the Soviet Union, the forcible relocations and mass killings in Cambodia—they either countered that the United States had been guilty of comparable sins or that these regimes had been driven to extreme measures precisely to fight American imperialism. Fewer people take this position today, but I often see the same phenomenon played out with different labels: Harmful statements and actions by women are dismissed as provoked and justified by toxic masculinity; by people of color as provoked and legitimated by toxic whiteness. It's not that human actions are never deformed by the distortions of a dominant force. Those provocations are real. It's just that even under such conditions, human beings have agency and

choice in how to respond. No doubt politics are easier if you know who the Great Satan is, but sacrificing the ability to see the world in all its contradictions and complexity seems a high price to pay for ease.

In the eighties, though, this consensus on the Left—that all must be forgiven (or at least overlooked) because all is overdetermined by American imperialism—I found hard to resolve. Maybe my friends were right. The United States' misdeeds were many and massive. Who were we to point fingers at its opponents? But I could no more immunize oppressive governments from criticism with this rationale than I could join Sontag in singing the praises of *Reader's Digest.* (She later backpedaled on that one.) Neither did I wish to be an apologist for regimes that had done so much harm to their own people.

I was shortly rescued from this dilemma by Isaiah Berlin.

Berlin was born the son of a Jewish timber baron in what was soon to become the Republic of Latvia. He fled with his family to England after the 1917 revolution. By age twelve, he was fluent in English. He excelled both in private school and at Oxford. He taught at Oxford for the rest of his life, winning many honors while maintaining that he was not an English philosopher but a Latvian Jew, a marked departure from the assimilationist expectations of many British intellectuals. I wonder if these two distinct identities contributed to his love of pluralism, where values contend and, through a process of compromise, political thought and action advance. He drew on a quotation from Kant as the title of one of his books: "Out of the crooked timber

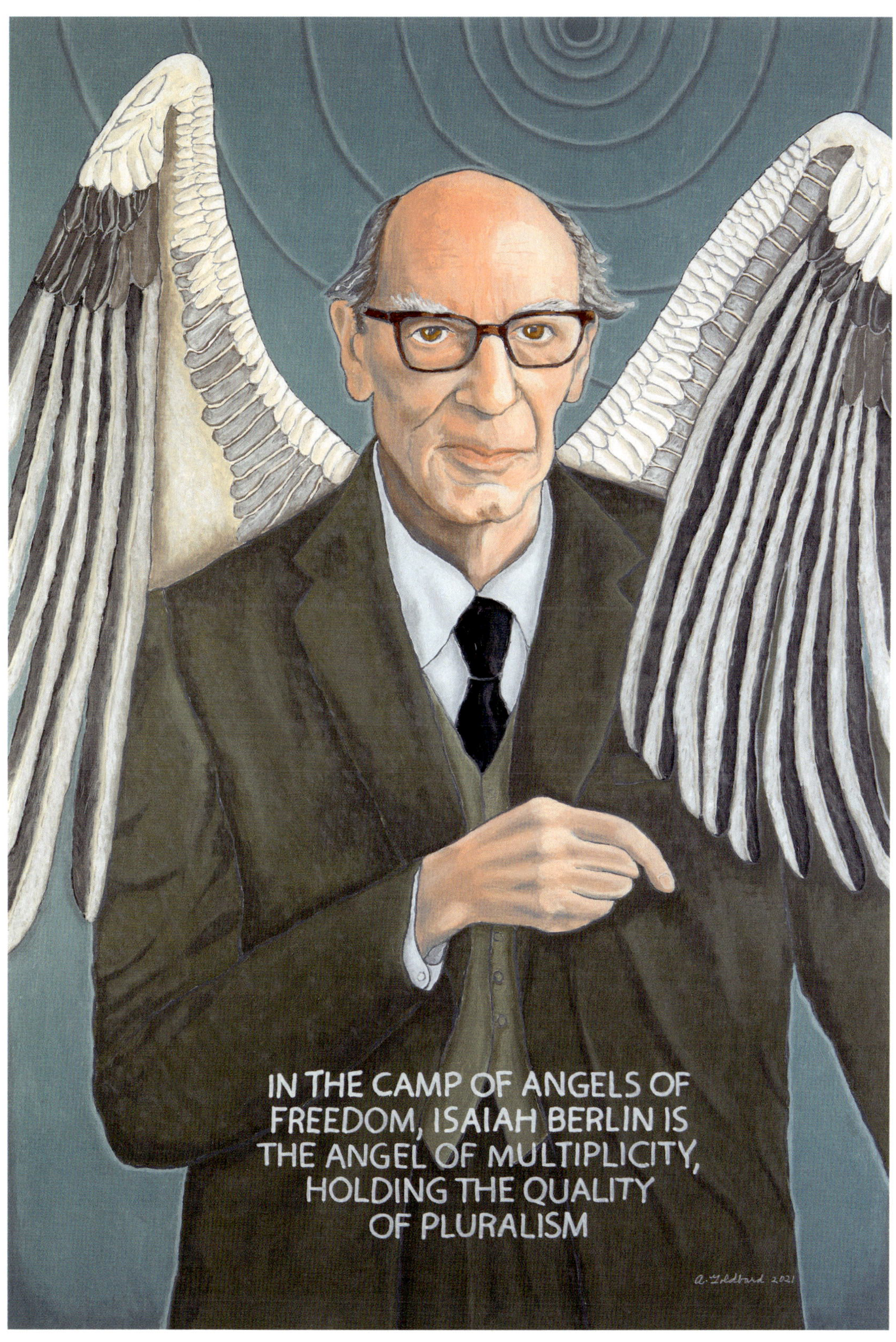
IN THE CAMP OF ANGELS OF
FREEDOM, ISAIAH BERLIN IS
THE ANGEL OF MULTIPLICITY,
HOLDING THE QUALITY
OF PLURALISM

of humanity no straight thing was ever made."

The insight Berlin gained from his study of history gave me a resolve that has never since wavered. When I was going along with the crowd in defending left-wing certainties and turning a blind eye to crimes committed in their name, I was an ideologue. A scrim of principles and conclusions lay between me and the world, so I was able to perceive reality only insofar as it conformed to or validated my preexisting understanding. But Berlin convinced me to question all ideology, and my questioning persuaded me to abandon the stance of an ideologue altogether. It seemed to me—and still does—that it is more possible to achieve what my angel Abraham Joshua Heschel called "an authentic awareness" by looking without preconception at all that can be discerned.

This is wonderfully expressed in a pair of phrases coined by Berlin. He called the big, obvious stuff of human events the "clear layer." If you look only at the clear layer of visible events, ideology is easy: You study a chronology of, say, certain wars, and from that deduce a general theory of war. The trouble is, no general theory of war fits or explains all wars, nor have any of them offered much foresight about how to prevent the next war. But they do lead to disputes in which theories contend, generating little value except for the careers of historians.

Beneath this is the much thicker "dark layer," which I think of as a name for the aggregate of our individual stories, made up of "less and less obvious yet more and more intimate and pervasive characteristics, too

closely mixed with feelings and activities to be easily distinguishable from them. . . ." Without the subtle meanings revealed in dreams, gestures, metaphors, and feelings, comprehension is absurdly shallow.

I found this utterly convincing. Berlin asked us to imagine who would be better able to predict an individual's responses to a given situation, a professional, such as a psychologist, who has been supplied with a huge amount of data about that individual, or someone who happens to know that person well. I have no doubt of the answer.

Berlin was greatly disturbed by society's failure to recognize this truth. Having observed the aftermath of the Russian Revolution, the rise of fascism—the proliferation and power of ideologies based on believing that humans can be shaped into an orderly machine guided by a set of inviolable principles—he thought we ought to be able to see through this lie. So many theories of human behavior are stated in terms better suited to the physical sciences, defending a generalization about human beings as if we were as easily measured as rocks or gases, claiming scientific certainty in predicting how people will behave. For Berlin and for me, this is grotesque. The human subject cannot be reduced to an equation.

Observing how the Russian Revolution had proclaimed "a new man," then slaughtered countless old ones to make room, drowning egalitarian ideas in an ocean of blood, Berlin rejected utopian notions that attempted to make human beings in all our differences conform to an ideological template. This moved me with tremendous force. I wondered why I had not previously sat down to contemplate what, despite their differences, the French Revolution, the Russian Revolution, and the American Revolution had in common—which was the conviction that a great many corpses were needed to establish freedom for the people left standing. Whether authoritarian ideologies ruled from the Right or the Left mattered little if the end result was the same.

Berlin wrote well about the practice of politics, praising politicians whose "sense of reality" equipped them to collaborate, compromise, to gauge opinion and opportunity and act accordingly. He is often placed in the "tragic romantic" camp, understanding that the best we can do is remain aware of the irrationality that suffuses human events, thus inoculating ourselves against grand theories purporting to rationalize them.

I encountered Berlin's work in the early eighties, when my body rebelled against the stresses I had heaped on it. I was laid up with painful back spasms and plenty of time to read. Dave and I had just returned to California after a few years in and around Washington, D.C. In the waning days of the Carter administration, we had been invited by a coalition of cultural activists to codirect a national network for the community arts field. Sadly, the Reagans arrived just as we were settling, and the landscape changed from cloth coats and public access to furs and daily police roadblocks to make way for luxury motorcades. The far-right Heritage Foundation became the new administration's official think tank, and on its advice, the public programs that had supported the work of community-based artists across the United States were defunded with remarkable rapidity.

We networked and organized and churned out newsletters, creating templates on an IBM Selectric typewriter. (Here's a time anchor: Our first personal computer was purchased on our return to California in 1983.) We were ejected by guards from public meetings at agencies such as the National Endowment for the Arts (NEA), where sunshine laws were no longer deemed relevant. We continued writing and speaking about cultural democracy—pluralism, participation, and equity in cultural policy and practice—and were repeatedly denounced for it. In one memorable meeting of the National Council on the Arts (the NEA's presidentially appointed governing body), actor and folksinger Theodore Bikel, who was deemed a liberal, denounced the concept of cultural democracy as "an autocracy of the uninformed—cultural democracy meaning we have to be dictated to by those for whom we toil. . . . The monies and efforts of this agency are not meant for the people of the United States, they are meant for artists of excellence. . . ."

In this climate, funding for community-based arts was scarcer than ever. Dave and I tried to support our organizing work by taking consulting jobs and tithing back to our putative employer. We facilitated national conversations that showed how people were coping, interviewing dozens of artists and cultural activists and collating their comments into a kind of round-robin dialogue. We learned that people were confused, sometimes desperate. Through a comedy of errors I can't quite reproduce, the future of our group was put in the hands of a man with some vague connection with the CIA (really!), who said he'd lost the documents we needed to continue.

Before long, we gave up and returned to California. I read Berlin in the apartment we'd rented in San Francisco's Sunset District. The streetcar rattled by every few minutes, beginning at 5:00 A.M. When the noise awakened me, I levered myself out of bed and lay on the bedroom floor with my knees supported on pillows, hoping that would fix my back. What it fixed first was my addiction to ideology and the way it blurred my vision.

When I took off the mask of ideology, I experienced a deep feeling of liberation. I no longer had to condemn people or acts just because they emanated from "the other side." I no longer had to approve all the positions taken by "our side." I could proceed with open eyes, weighing alternatives in light of the fullness of the human subject, rather than through the lens of cold logic, which excludes so much. My spirit lightened. My thoughts were freer.

In this country today, the Right exemplifies Berlin's warnings, escalating calls for censorship, for bloodshed, for a revolution that cements white supremacy. On the Left, I have observed related tendencies closest to hand. I've had ample opportunity to practice freedom from ideology, and have often been criticized for it. For example, as #MeToo emerged, many of the people with whom I engage in political discussion took to declaring the slogan "Believe women." There is ample evidence that few false reports of sexual harassment or worse misconduct are made, so both reason and feeling say to give such accusations full

weight. But to assert that *no* false reports are made is patently untrue. Punishment without any attempt to verify accusations can lead to a form of persecution reminiscent of the Red Scare, when Senator Joseph McCarthy ended livelihoods and lives merely by waving a sheaf of papers. But when I said this, I was denounced, most often by young activists who had little knowledge of the fifties witch hunts but boundless faith in their own intuition.

Of all my angels, Berlin made one of the biggest differences in my life because he introduced me to ideas that radically altered my worldview and behavior, freeing me from the grip of an ideology that falsified my values, and strengthening my ability to think for myself. Reading Berlin, I faced unsettling truths. I am sometimes worried about the orthodoxies rampant in certain sectors of the Left, such as the proclivity to see race as a natural truth, not as the social construct it is, imposed as an instrument of white supremacy. I am saddened by the essentialism that too often equates skin color or gender with virtue and fails to give economic inequality its full value in forging coalitions of people who are not the same but have enough in common to gather strength in numbers if only ideological obstacles were not such an impediment. I wish people would question assumptions and move toward a sense of reality that makes room for compromise without betraying core values of equity, love, justice, belonging. I think Berlin would have joined me in doubting that I will get my wish.

9

John Trudell

*In the Camp of Angels of Freedom, John Trudell is the Angel of
Heartbroken Hope, holding the quality of yearning.*

It may seem strange that the writer and Indigenous activist John Trudell, who was made to feel unwelcome in so many ways, would turn my thoughts toward belonging. But it makes perfect sense. Though Trudell was marooned in a society founded on exploitation through separation, his life—his music, writing, his way of living— reclaimed an understanding of existence in which everything is connected. All are related. Everyone belongs.

I first heard Trudell's name when he appeared as spokesperson for the 1969–1971 occupation of Alcatraz by Native Americans who claimed treaty rights to the island when the federal prison closed. I heard it again when he took on the chair of the American Indian Movement in 1973. But I didn't hear his music till much later.

The challenge and beauty of his calling came to my attention exactly when I needed it, when I was walking the razor's edge between taking refuge in otherness and trying to belong.

I was in my forties, living—miserably but stuck fast for years to come—with my second husband, Dave, in Ukiah, California, the seat of Mendocino County, less than two hours north of San Francisco. The marriage was fed by our desperate desire to belong. Unseen, unloved, miserable in our own families, and uneasy in every role we'd been assigned, we found refuge in each other. For a time, it worked. We thought entering into a kind of fusion could heal the harm our families had done, so whenever discord threatened, we drew the ties that bound us even tighter. Moving was always our chief distraction, deflecting attention that would otherwise have gone to the increasingly suffocating state of our marriage. At the end of the eighties, we'd gotten a large contract for a cultural planning project, which gave us enough capital to move from San Francisco to a rural community that fit our desires: a garden and quiet, where we could both write and I could paint.

We got our wish. We wrote a book about cultural democracy, which was never published. Inspired by M. F. K. Fisher, I wrote a memoir with recipes and the first of several novels, also never published. I painted a series of portraits of friends, each including an image of Earth's globe, as in the self-portrait I wrote about in my essay on Alice Neel. In one, a crystal ball Earth sits in the lap of a self-styled guru; in another, the Earth is tucked like a helmet under the arm of a knight wearing armor and running shoes. Those pictures are gone now. When many years later I left Dave, he promised to keep them safe until I could fetch them, but he made them disappear. I sometimes wonder if he got the idea from my mother.

We'd picked Ukiah, the seat of Mendocino County, because it was affordable, a bearable two-hour commute to San Francisco International Airport, and because we had friends and colleagues there. When we'd worked for the California Arts Council, we'd connected with local people who'd started arts groups—a community theater, a local arts council. They directed us to Mara, a woman who had arrived a decade earlier as part of a back-to-the-land homestead movement, and who'd recently bought a place in town so that her daughter could attend the local high school. While we lived in the main house and learned rural lifeways from our landlady, she and her daughter stayed in the guest cottage in the back. Mara was an incredibly knowledgeable and skillful environmental activist, so renting her house led to our being involved in projects to save the old-growth forests.

Moving to a small town shone a light on my perpetual dilemma—wanting to belong, always feeling other. Everyone we met knew everyone else, often very well, making it a challenge to keep track of which

parents went with which children, which partners currently fit together, as opposed to having once been a couple, but no longer. It seemed that knowing you've been planted in a small orchard led to conviviality, because despite breakups and other dislocations, people remained in connection, shifting from something like lovers to something like cousins. The fluidity of these relationships made me question the locked-room quality of our own.

We were invited to gatherings but seldom introduced to anyone. There was no malice in it: Didn't everyone know each other already? Once we'd met people, though, they dropped in unannounced whenever they felt like it. They made it clear that our wish to receive a call first was a lingering artifact of bourgeois society, like finger bowls. I often felt at a loss for what to say or how to behave. Still, as time passed, I made true and steadfast friends there, including three women I have talked with once a month for the last thirty years.

I soon learned that I could connect by offering my skills. In that part of Northern California, timber had long been king, employing large numbers, financing and influencing elected officials, claiming social and political power commensurate with the industry's economic power. By the end of the eighties, two trends were upsetting this long-standing state of affairs. Forests had been depleted by overharvesting, so timber companies were moving to the Global South, where wood was plentiful, wages low, and environmental regulations practically nonexistent. At the same time, young people had since the seventies moved in greater and greater numbers to rural

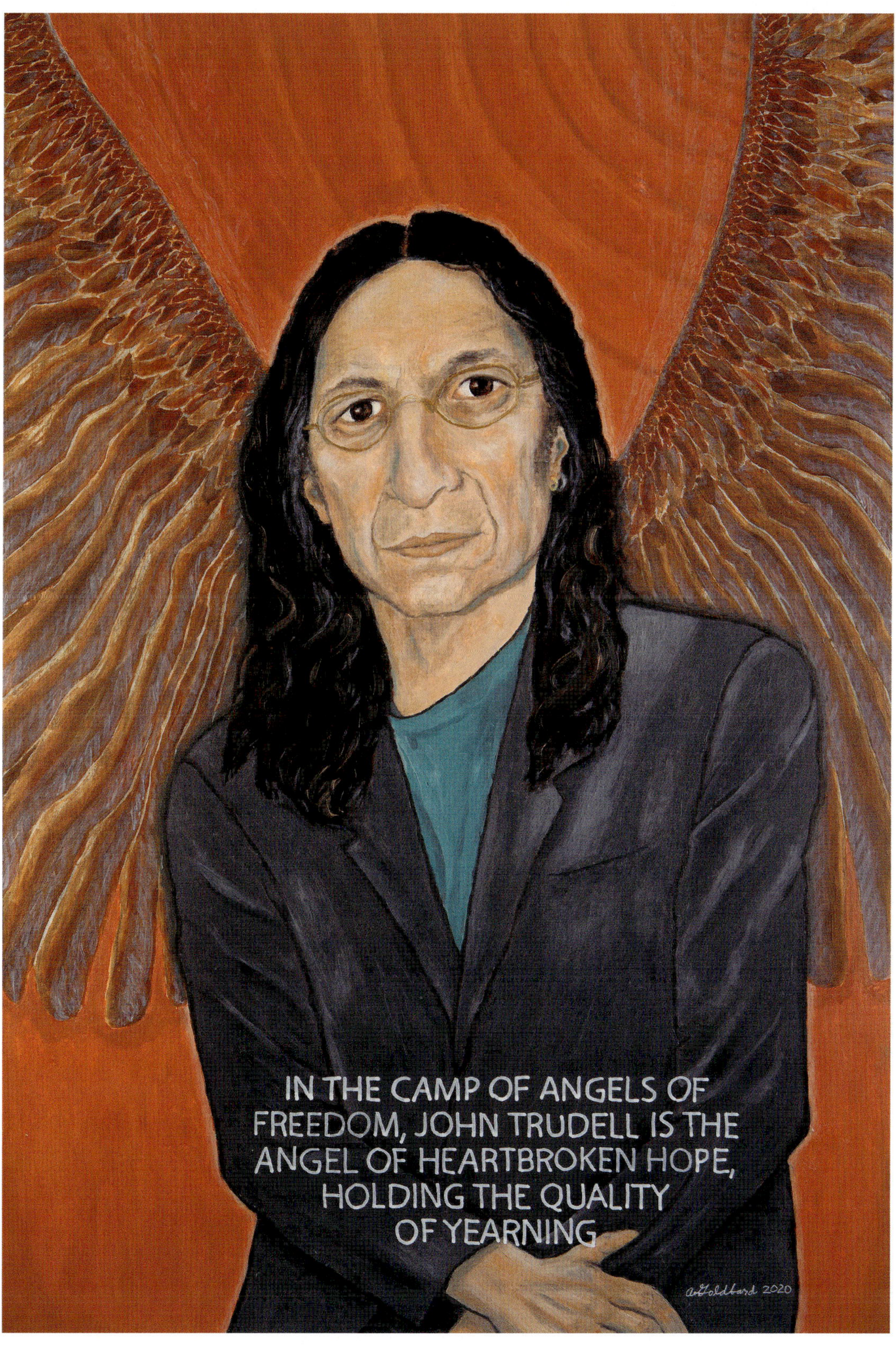

IN THE CAMP OF ANGELS OF
FREEDOM, JOHN TRUDELL IS THE
ANGEL OF HEARTBROKEN HOPE,
HOLDING THE QUALITY
OF YEARNING

communities like ours, where land was relatively cheap and abundant. They wanted to escape what they saw as the decline of cities, to turn their backs on extractive economies and create a cooperative and environmentally gentle way of life.

Around the time we met her, Mara had been appointed by the county Board of Supervisors to an advisory panel created to scrutinize existing timber-harvest regulations and recommend needed changes. Her fellow panel members included other activists, representatives of public agencies, and timber corporation executives. The playing field wasn't exactly level: Timber executives and representatives from agencies such as the Forest Service collected their salaries and expenses while they took part; activists had to draw on their own time and resources, usually scarce. But everyone agreed to the terms of engagement.

After a multiyear deliberative process, the panel was stymied. Environmental and agency members had come up with a plan to limit timber harvests to a "percentage of inventory" that would save old-growth forests and support replanting and replenishment, leading to long-term sustainable harvesting. The timber companies seemed open to it, although never quite ready to act. Many compromises were adopted, with each side declaring a willingness to give something up on the way to agreement.

Then everything fell apart. The timber representatives claimed they'd been railroaded. They hired an industry-backed group advocating what they called "wise use" to provide strategic advice and messaging portraying environmentalists as job killers. When public hearings were scheduled to invite comment on the recommendations, the timber companies gave their employees the day off, equipped them with matching T-shirts, and bused them to the venue, where they were instructed to stamp their feet, drowning out whoever spoke in favor of the recommendations. Children of timber workers sent nearly identical handwritten letters to officials, pleading for their parents' jobs.

The Board of Supervisors asked Dave and me to design a deliberative process that would actually permit debate and consideration. We facilitated meetings of the panel where everyone had ample time and space to weigh in. They were broadcast live on public radio and cable-access channels. Videotapes were made available at local libraries, public agencies, and organizations. Everyone had a chance to hear all viewpoints, up close, without disruption. When the recommendations came to a vote, three of the five supervisors voted to reject them. Within a few years, the corporate timber companies had all pulled out and headed south, triggering the closing of sawmills and wood-based manufacturing. The workers who had loyally defended corporate interests were left behind and out of luck.

What I learned from this process seems directly transferable to U.S. politics today. Don't let your opponents make the rules, especially if all they need to win is to keep whatever you want from happening, while victory for you requires creating, persuading, and enacting new initiatives. Don't mistake delaying tactics for deliberation. Don't deceive yourself that two diametrically opposed interests can come to agreement, no matter how long they try.

I should have listened to John Trudell: "For decades, my identity was political, but I've come to understand that there's no political solution when you're dealing with someone else's rules."

Until I met Mara and the other homesteaders in Mendocino County, I'd thought of myself as countercultural. To me that meant politically radical, indifferent to convention, interested in whatever promised to alter consciousness. But our new friends gave it a much fuller meaning.

People lived off the grid, raised nearly all their own food, built their own houses, invented generator systems, tended roads and dams, grew dope in the hidden heights of the national forest, and were even more skeptical than I was about the long-term prospects of a society they had determined to leave behind. They were often also spectacularly credulous, burying pebbles in a certain configuration at a certain time of day to ensure the success of the Harmonic Convergence, a rare alignment of planets in 1987 that was supposed to bring peace; taking part in Ponzi schemes and so-called "sovereign citizen" lawsuits (unbeknownst to our friends, these were backed by white supremacists) claiming the federal government was illegitimate and owed compensation to each person filing suit. We were sometimes used as reality checks, having so recently come from the urban belly of the beast. But our neighbors' credulity didn't diminish their survival skills. From them we learned to compost food scraps, grow tomatoes, find mushrooms, follow local politics. And listen to John Trudell.

Trudell's questioning nature made him a local favorite. He spoke of Indigenous lifeways when it had become clear to the back-to-the-landers that the larger society's alienation from nature and tradition would come home to roost. He advocated legalizing marijuana and hemp growing at a time when most people in my generation understood the healing power of certain plants used in the right ways and the absurdity of alcohol-guzzling, pill-popping, tobacco- and sugar-addicted gatekeepers outlawing those plants. With respect to Indigenous cultural rights, wars of conquest, state surveillance, environmental despoliation, and a slew of other issues pitting free people against a controlling state, Trudell's reputation for fearless speech was well earned and well loved.

Mara invited us to a Trudell concert in Sonoma County, just to the south. Trudell was no singer, but the musicians he played with lifted his spoken-word compositions sky-high, especially the heart-wrenching guitar of the late Jesse Ed Davis, who can be heard on *AKA Grafitti Man*. That night, after the music ended, I sat in the near-empty auditorium, feeling my ears and my heart ring. My friends went backstage to give Trudell a perfect bud they had grown, but Dave didn't want to go. I still wish I had gone with them, had shaken Trudell's hand. Or maybe hugged him. Of all my angels, he is the one whose arms I most wanted to enter. He is the one who after death feels more flesh and blood than memory.

For me, Trudell embodied art's redemptive power. Among all his songs, I am most moved by "Tina Smiled," a beautiful tribute to his wife, Tina Manning, who died, along with their three children and her mother, in a house fire Trudell and

many others believed was politically motivated arson. Trudell didn't begin writing
poetry and lyrics until after his family was
killed. Life has taught me that such loss can
sometimes be made bearable by art. I can't
hear the song without my eyes filling.

My husband was alive, but our love was
on the way to lost. Dave was unmoored
from ordinary reality, including the safety
of his body, so that any day was likely to
bring a trip to the emergency room: slicing
his fingers while washing the knives, filling
a thermos with boiling water that spilled
over his hand, loosening the skin so that it
drooped like a too-large glove. What made
me stay was the stubborn conviction that
I could fix things, which I hung on to until
the level of rage and fear became intolerable, until it became clear that it would
be Dave's life or mine. As I held on, I put
"Tina Smiled" on repeat, wrapping myself

in yearning, imagining the warmth of being
held with open arms.

Trudell's story and mine couldn't have
been more different, but each led us to a
kind of belonging, the fellowship of those
who can never unsee the emperor's-new-
clothes absurdity of this society. Many talks
by Trudell are easily accessible on YouTube.
Watching them, I feel a kinship with the
earnestness of his attempts to explain this
society in a way that would break its hold
on the listener.

Trudell never stopped trying. From his
life and work, I learned to accept my own
alienation without judgment, yet never to
deny my own yearning to belong. I learned
to see myself as a kind of tuning fork,
vibrating in harmony with the possible, no
matter how improbable it might seem to
others. And eventually, I learned to let go.

10

Abraham Joshua Heschel

*In the Camp of Angels of Freedom, Abraham Joshua Heschel is the
Angel of Radical Amazement, holding the quality of wonder.*

I was brought up with a strong Jewish identity, mostly secular. My mother was born shortly after her parents arrived here from Russia, traveling by steamship. They fled the Cossacks, who had killed my great-grandfather, thereby evading my grandfather's being drafted into the czar's army, considered a death sentence for Jews. My grandmother had green eyes and red braids coiled over her ears—like Princess Leia. I was told that the ship's captain fell for her, tried to persuade her to leave her husband. I wonder if she ever regretted her refusal.

My father came from London—where his parents had emigrated from Poland—as a young man, looking for opportunity. I have an identity card he carried into this country. In the place where his nose should have been was something blurry, the result of his having been beaten daily by anti-Semitic thugs on his way from Whitechapel to the tailor shop where he apprenticed.

Like so many immigrants, my forebears were embraced by this country's secular Jewish Left, chiefly the Workmen's Circle (Arbeter Ring), which taught them to read and write in Yiddish, never to cross a picket line, and to place themselves on the side of the oppressed. My mother and her brother went to Arbeter Ring after-school classes. I have a photo of them as teenagers. Both resembled overstuffed chairs, evidently due to my grandmother's habit of taking treats to school each day to sustain their learning. There was a huge cohort of cousins. In the summer, they took excursions to an aunt's farm in New Jersey to play games and loll in the sun. When they got hungry, they pulled spring onions from the garden to layer with schmaltz on thick slices of rye bread. I realized how assimilated I was when an enthusiastic description of this snack upset my stomach.

My parents, aunt, uncle, and grandparents moved from New Jersey to California when I was not quite two years old. My grandfather had a heart attack, which was somehow kept secret from him, but not from anyone else. The doctor advised a retreat from the extreme weather of New York, which had peaked with the blizzard of 1947. My father arranged to be mustered out of the service in California and find us all a place to live. With my uncle driving a carful of women—one pregnant—excuses were contrived to cut each day's journey short. This was supposed to save my grandfather the stress of long days on the road, but he was greatly agitated by the trip's slow pace, so the plan backfired. My uncle, even more impatient, was in charge of the home-movie camera. There's a hilarious movie consisting of a dozen or so fifteen-second shots of notable locations: Don't blink or you'll miss Mount Rushmore.

All my memories of Jewish holidays take place in the small Northern California suburban house my parents and grandparents shared. They are all the same: a houseful of noisy people, a big meal focusing on festive foods, just a token acknowledgment of the religious occasion.

It wasn't until I was fifty or so that I began to crave something more than my family's cultural identification with Jewish history. I can pinpoint the exact moment, the very end of 1997. Dave and I were on a vacation in Kauai. It rained every day and I ran out of reading material. A new chain bookstore had opened in Lihue. The store had a large Judaica section (they must have equipped all their new stores with the same inaugural stock; that section shrank each time I visited). My plan to browse was confounded when a book seized my attention.

The Thirteen-Petalled Rose was a slim volume by Rabbi Adin Steinsaltz, a straightforward account of a subject that is anything but: Jewish mysticism. I had no particular interest in the subject. I hadn't heard of the author—I later learned he was

a hugely respected scholar. But no matter how widely I ranged in the enormous store, my feet kept pulling me back to *The Thirteen-Petalled Rose.* I could not leave without buying it. When we returned to the place we'd rented, I read the book in one long sitting, mesmerized. It was New Year's Eve. We went out for a special dinner during which I narrated the entire book.

I felt as if the deck of my life had been reshuffled. Before I read *The Thirteen-Petalled Rose,* I'd been depressed, feeling as if my life had been a punishment for crimes unknown. But Steinsaltz asserted that every person has a place in life analogous to each letter in the Torah, a unique task to perform that cannot be predicted but must be embraced when it arrives.

I instantly understood that what I had perceived as punishment should be seen instead as preparation. Everything shifted.

When we returned home to California, I contacted everyone I knew who was more knowledgeable than I about Jewish texts and practices, asking their advice. Now that I had this insight, how should I live? The first book anyone sent me was Rabbi Abraham Joshua Heschel's *The Sabbath.*

It's a long story from there. As soon as I finished one of the Jewish books friends had shared, Dave picked it up and read it. His study convinced him that he was Jewish, which jibed with his persistent feeling of not belonging to the vaguely Protestant world in which he'd grown up. It also made spiritual sense to some of the teachers of mysticism we read. They pointed out that there had not been enough Jewish bodies to contain the six million souls murdered in the Holocaust, so it was unsurprising

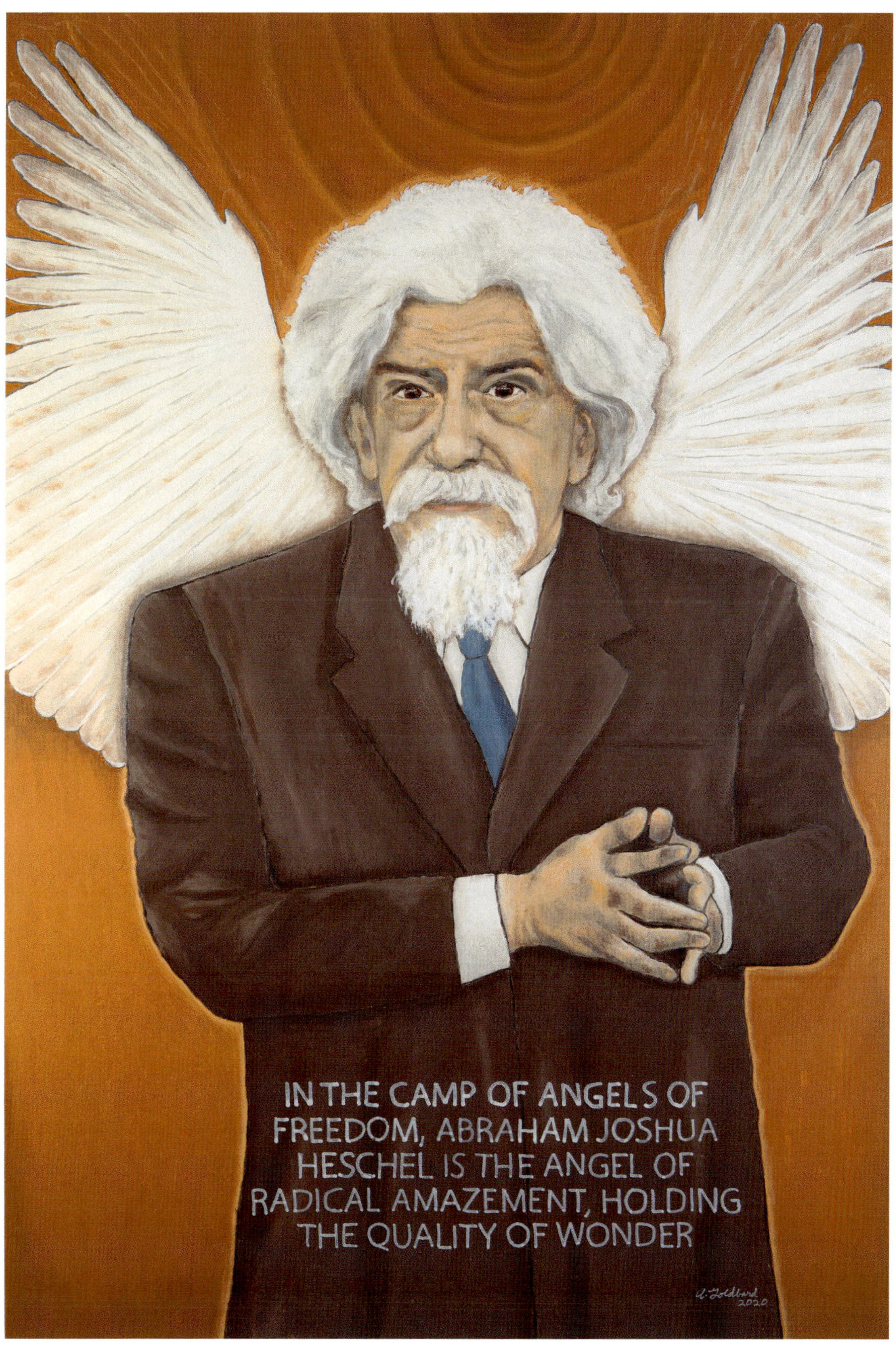
IN THE CAMP OF ANGELS OF
FREEDOM, ABRAHAM JOSHUA
HESCHEL IS THE ANGEL OF
RADICAL AMAZEMENT, HOLDING
THE QUALITY OF WONDER

that many non-Jews of our generation had been drawn to what felt like a lost identity, hosting Jewish souls. *Lovesong: Becoming A Jew,* the memoir of conversion by author and civil rights activist Julius Lester, convinced us this was real.

Dave wanted to study for conversion and I wanted to live in a larger Jewish community. We settled on Seattle and met a remarkable rabbi, who welcomed us. When it turned out that he had been a visiting rabbi in our tiny Northern California town before taking his congregational job in Seattle, I felt we had been destined to connect. He changed my life in the short year before he died in an automobile accident—right after asking me to assume the presidency of the community, clearly more on account of my organizational experience than my knowledge of Judaism. His death propelled me into an intensive course in Jewish practice, as it fell to me to help console and sustain our small community. That led to deep involvement in the flavor of Judaism known as "Jewish renewal," which might be summed up as feminism meets Hasidism: ecstatic, egalitarian, inclusive, creative.

In my great thirst for Jewish learning, rooted in both practical and spiritual desire, I read other books by Rabbi Heschel. *Who Is Man?* offered a description of my awakening in Kauai: "This is the most important experience in the life of every human being: something is asked of me. Every human being has had a moment in which he sensed a mystery waiting for him. Meaning is found in responding to the demand, meaning is found in sensing the demand."

Heschel's central insight struck me with profound force. He saw wonder, which

in this spiritual context he called "radical amazement," as a refusal to adjust to the default reality that pretends to explain everything but actually substitutes conventional notions for full, present, open awareness. Instead of premade answers to life's great questions, he offered relationship to the mystery of existence. This contradicts the conventional idea of science as the antidote to religion. Convinced atheists often say that as scientific knowledge grows, belief will become less and less sustainable. While I sometimes envy their certainty, I can't imagine that what science tells us about *how* the physical world works will ever tell us *why* it exists. That inquiry is the province of spiritual thought and practice.

Heschel led me to see spiritual practice not as separate from my political and cultural work or other aspects of ordinary life, but as deeply entwined with them. I have a photo on my office wall of Rabbi Heschel marching with Dr. Martin Luther King, Jr., from Selma to Montgomery. King, Heschel, and Ralph Bunche walk arm in arm, each of them wearing a lei supplied in solidarity by the Reverend Abraham Akaka from Hawaii. Recalling that day, Heschel said, "I felt my legs were praying."

My work at the time I first encountered Heschel involved artists cocreating with community members. Some made plays based on first-person accounts gathered from people affected by an issue. Through collecting and crafting such stories, the abstraction of the prison-industrial complex, for example—the fact that ours is the largest prison population, the most punishing system on the planet, implicating all of us— became a nexus of human stories, deeply real, touching, and activating. Others made works of public art depicting a community's history or aspirations through its members' eyes, or poetic manifestos weaving many people's words and voices into an engaging tapestry.

When I began to see this work as a form of spiritual practice, its value was amplified and renewed. In acts of artistic co-creation, people are both most themselves and most God-like, bringing into being the world they desire. When children—who at school have already been told too often to sit down and shut up—are invited to make their marks, contributing to a collective portrait of their own experiences, their faces open like sunlit flowers. Such work unearths suffering, to be sure, yet it also offers glimpses of a perfected world, much like the tales that make up every faith's sacred texts. When I was working with people to express their concerns or hopes through art, I saw myself as practicing freedom. For me, that is the fulfillment of spirit.

Every type of work exists in a context that can support or distort it. In the dominant society, where value must be quantified and tender feelings are not supposed to intrude on the world of action, community artists are expected to see their work not primarily as spiritually enlarging, but in an entirely different way. According to this reductive perspective, the people they create with are deficient and the remedy is to make them change, promoting recommended forms of self-improvement and social conformity. But for practitioners, the true intention of the work, as of all spiritual practice, is to soften the conventional world into opening its eyes and ears in what Heschel called "authentic awareness." The work pursues change, but it is a change in the minds and hearts of those who feel entitled to prescribe correction for people with less social power, when what they actually need is to be truly heard and seen.

Offering talks and workshops has been a big part of my work. I've repeatedly argued that making art is intrinsic to human life: Our earliest ancestors painted in caves; today, people in the most terrible conditions risk their safety to make drawings on prison walls, to dance in detention camps, to pass forbidden writings from hand to hand.

In 2006, I was invited to keynote the conference of the National Guild for Community Arts Education, an alliance of community music schools, art workshops, and so on—all of them challenged to find support in times that undervalued such work. When I read that the organization's founding director had led a clandestine orchestra in the Dachau concentration camp, I began to tremble. I realized that I must use this speaking opportunity to express what I had been seeing. Conventionally, the work of the people I would address might be understood as training the unskilled, delivering social services, or running a business—all valid, practical frameworks, if inadequate to hold the totality of the work. But I hoped that seeing it as spiritual practice would be empowering.

Yet I was afraid. Many people I knew were allergic to religion, shutting down at the slightest mention of spirituality. I wasn't planning to foist dogma on anyone. In fact, the texts I shared were ecumenical, their authors ranging from Gandhi to Thich Nhat Hanh to Rebbe Nachman of Breslov to the Reverend Dr. Martin Luther King, Jr., to the Sufi mystic Rumi. But in quoting those spiritual teachers, I was offering my audience a different lens from those commonly used to view the work. I was going to frame it as inviting radical amazement.

On the day of my address, I felt especially anxious. My heart pounded as I took to the dais. But when I began to speak, something shifted. I hadn't known beforehand that I would be giving people a story of their work that lifted doubts, that reflected back to them its real and lasting value, a story mainstream institutions refused to acknowledge but which had been held and cherished in a secretly hopeful hiding place by every person in the room. By the time I had finished, people were weeping openly. I was so happy I'd taken the risk.

My relationship to spiritual practice has changed many times since that rainy day I ran out of things to read on Kauai. The process of learning from Jewish texts and teachers and pouring what I'd learned into service to the community in Seattle was spiritually intoxicating for me. I had the feeling I was being watched over. The membrane between material and spiritual worlds became very thin. In a 1958 sermon, Dr. King expressed what I felt: "Everything that we see is a shadow cast by that which we do not see." I loved those feelings, which seemed a kind of grace. Spiritual teachers talk about basic trust, a foundational sense of being held by the universe. Those days were the only time I have ever experienced it.

But I now see this was a developmental stage, expressing a parental relationship—unsustainable for me in maturity—with life's mystery. The more I interacted with actu-

ally existing spiritual leaders, the more a twist of disillusionment insinuated itself past my sense of protection. Just as I discovered as a young person that an artist's brilliance was no guarantee of that person's goodness, I was sad to realize that some of the teachers I'd encountered who'd been marinating in spiritual study and practice for decades were not prevented by it from sexually exploiting students, deceiving those closest to them, or committing other ethical transgressions.

What has stayed with me is an understanding I took from Heschel's 1969 essay "On Prayer." "Prayer is meaningless unless it is subversive," he wrote, "unless it seeks to overthrow and to ruin the pyramids of callousness, hatred, opportunism, falsehoods. The liturgical movement must become a revolutionary movement, seeking to overthrow the forces that continue to destroy the promise, the hope, the vision."

From Abraham Joshua Heschel, I learned to notice and feel gratitude for the many moments of radical amazement punctuating even ordinary days: the times that stopping to gaze at a beloved or into the heart of a rose ignites an awareness that can never be fully expressed but which artists and others must never abandon trying to convey. I owe him a debt for the many times I have noticed that I've allowed conventional notions and mental clichés to cloud my awareness of what is, and have returned to open-eyed presence. He allowed me to experience the realization every day offers, that even the most ordinary or banal acts can be lifted into the realm of spiritual practice by a simple refusal to adjust to default reality.

11

Jane Jacobs

*In The Camp of Angels of Freedom, Jane Jacobs is the Angel
of Lived Knowledge, holding the quality of seeing without assumption.*

A decade or so ago, I was struggling to find a way to frame a book on autodidacts—I called it "The Auto Club"—when a friend, shocked that I hadn't included the original thinker and writer Jane Jacobs, told me I had to read her best-known book immediately. This was *The Death and Life of Great American Cities,* published in 1961. Discovering Jane Jacobs was like happening on a long-lost family member—not my actually existing family, mind you, but a clan of true belonging, of autodidacts and uncolonized minds.

I had been grappling for years with the contradictions, the challenges, of my own position as a minor public intellectual, as an adviser and frequent speaker in a world that prized credentialed expertise over lived knowledge. The qualities I brought to my professional and political roles seemed to mask my actual story. People made assumptions about me that weren't true, assumptions that served only to reinforce their prejudices. If I was intelligent, articulate, competent, I must also have come from privilege. I wanted to remove the mask, but Freire had shown me the extent to which I'd internalized the oppressor's voice. After so many years, I still carried a fear of being declared illegitimate.

I forced myself to defy my fear. I had been part of many meetings in which entitlement was called out, underpinned by the blithe assumption that everyone in the room shared the speaker's own privileges. I liked bursting the bubble of any self-righteous critic who would stand before the assembled to say "All of us went to college, all of us were given a leg up by our families, but what about who isn't in the room?" I liked to look such people in the eye and say, "Your class bias is showing." I would remind them they knew nothing about the actual lives of the individuals they addressed, that what they had to say was shaped by the knee-jerk assumption that most forms of intellectual mastery were attributes of class.

Of all the commonplace injustices that had ignited my empathy and outrage, the seldom questioned proclivity to treat the culling mechanism of a college degree as an ultimate indicator of value and entitlement to a voice—the unfairness of this lodged in my heart and mind. I couldn't abide the way this society wastes the intelligence and experience of working-class people who lack such credentials. I couldn't stand the ordinary elitism, the unacknowledged class bias, that colored even the most trivial interactions. I never falsified or hid my biography. My experience had granted me an exception to the rule, as I had spoken at enough colleges, published enough books and journal articles, received enough acknowledgment never to be questioned on my qualifications. So I wasn't significantly disadvantaged by my lack of formal credentials. But being treated as an exception was nowhere near enough to satisfy my desire for equity, reciprocity, and fairness for the multitudes who do suffer from credentialism.

For a while, I collected fellow autodidacts. Silicon Valley had a slew of dropout zillionaires. Literary history was peppered with autodidacts—Jorge Luis Borges, Richard Wright, William Faulkner—as were the worlds of film and politics. Some of my angels—Toulouse-Lautrec, Nina Simone, James Baldwin—also belonged to the auto club.

The autodidact I most loved discovering was Jane Jacobs, whose native wit, acute vision, kind heart, and faith in possibility were not (and could never have been) acquired at an institution of higher education.

From the first page of *The Death and Life of Great American Cities,* Jacobs's commitment to open-eyed observation thrilled me. She knew what she saw and had confidence in her perception. Her confidence

excited me, authorizing my own. She knew that despite the orthodoxies shaping fields that interested her—architecture and urban planning, as well as economics and politics—what she had to say carried a ring of undeniable truth, no matter how insistently it was challenged by her archenemy, Robert Moses, and others whose idea of progress entailed wiping out neighborhoods to make room for freeways, and who repeatedly dismissed her as a "housewife." I was delighted by her audacity and humaneness.

I admired the way her close observations of her Greenwich Village neighbors, their organic patterns of street life and relationship, slid seamlessly into a devastating critique of the type of urban planning that had given us high-rise public housing replete with danger and decline but utterly and intrinsically lacking the street-level humanity of true homes. I appreciated the special scorn she reserved for big cold ideas such as Le Corbusier's "Radiant City," where abstraction and conceptual elegance replaced the need for kindness and fellow feeling. She stuck a fork in the urban planning establishment: Turn them over and take them out; they're done!

Immersing myself in Jacobs's writing kept me grounded at a time when everything else in my life was contingent. It took me decades, but after a long and complicated final act, I ran out of trying with Dave and returned to California and caring friends. It felt like starting from scratch. In our final years, Dave had found, then lost half a dozen excellent jobs; his solution was to live on home equity until we had to sell our house. I came away after more than thirty years of marriage with a few

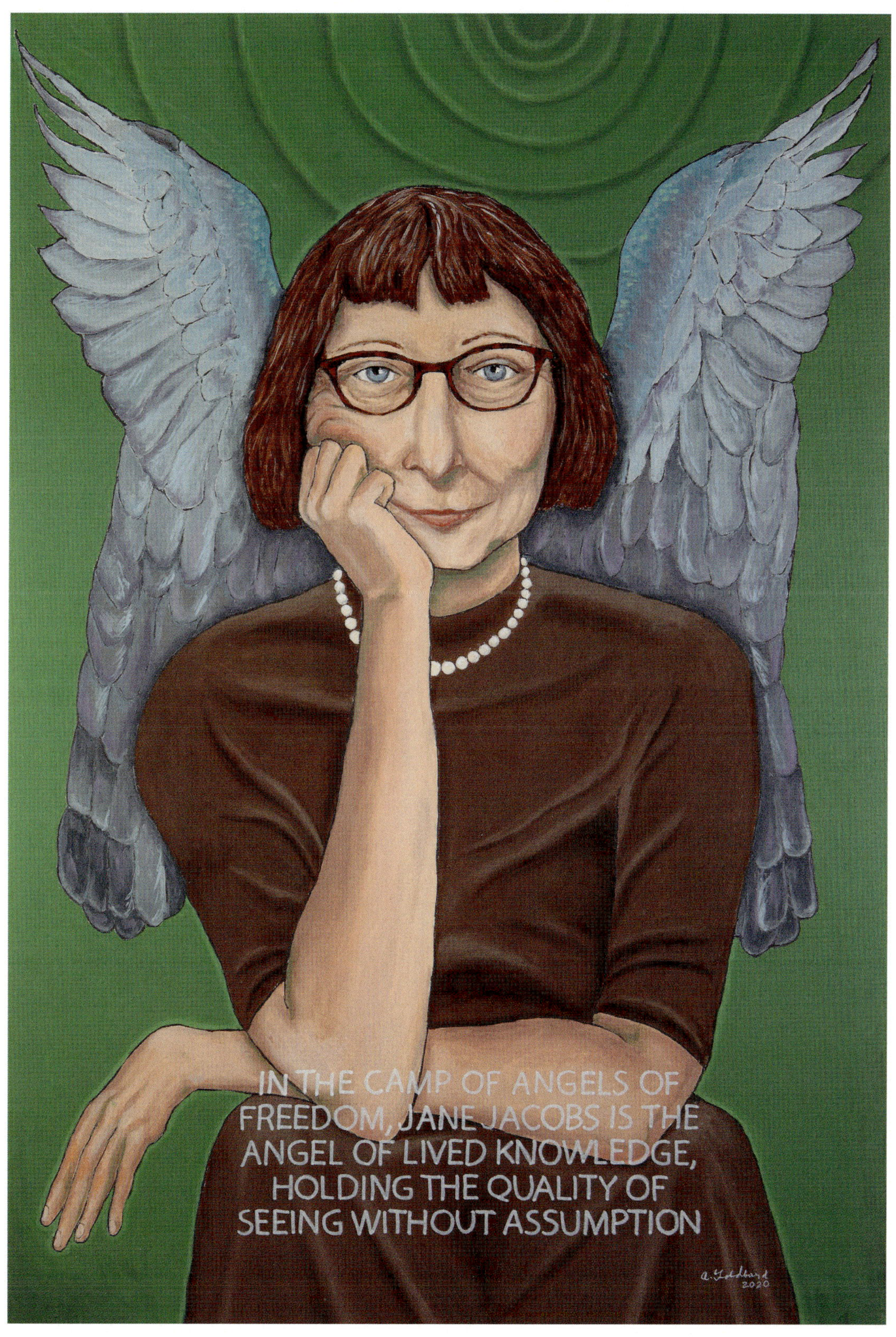
IN THE CAMP OF ANGELS OF
FREEDOM, JANE JACOBS IS THE
ANGEL OF LIVED KNOWLEDGE,
HOLDING THE QUALITY OF
SEEING WITHOUT ASSUMPTION

thousand dollars and most of my personal possessions. I wish I had insisted on more of the latter. I still dream of once again watching the only extant home movie of my father, the scene where he pries the lid off an enormous pot of *tcholent,* Ashkenazi Jews' traditional overnight Shabbos stew, inhaling with every cell of his body. But Dave refused to return it to me.

I threw myself into work, a lot of consulting and public speaking and just as much writing. I was asked to contribute a chapter to a New Village Press anthology in tribute to Jacobs, *What We See,* published in 2010. My essay comprised nine sections, each offering a different lens for looking at both cities and ourselves. They were subtitled "The Lens of the Uncolonized Mind," "The Lens of Language," "The Lens of Embedded Beliefs," "The Lens of Negative Liberty," and so on. It isn't that I was unaware of these lenses before I encountered Jacobs—indeed, two of them turn on the ideas of my angels Isaiah Berlin and Paul Goodman—but that her work, weaving a single fabric from both the ordinary and commonsensical and life's largest questions, made me feel that how I see the world may have something useful to offer.

Under the heading "The Lens of Common Fate," I wrote about planners' and policymakers' penchant for prescribing measures for others that they themselves would find intolerable. I pointed to Jacobs's characterization of the wholesale practice of relocation, which she called "slum shifting" and "slum duplicating." I loved the way she wrote about such absurdities as the then commonplace practice of public housing authorities who, forced to admit that a

housing project had failed, tried to address the failure by moving people into a new one just like it.

Inspired by Jacobs, I began to rely on a simple thought experiment I've always found useful in vetting policies and plans. Would those who make decisions about how others will live be willing to subject themselves and their families to the same strictures for a meaningful stretch of time? Sometimes in a public talk or workshop, I ask people to consider what might happen if policymakers' families had to make do with the medical care they prescribe for users of the public health system; or send their children to the poorest of the schools shaped by their policies; or sleep night after night amid the sounds, smells and other sensations of public housing. That this commonsense question is almost never asked—and earns a huge laugh on the few occasions when it is—is the true absurdity.

This perspective distinguishes Jane Jacobs from nearly every other angel who has inspired my life: Hers was a homely type of caring, fueled by empathy for her own children, her neighbors, and all whose lives she could touch or imagine. Her work makes clear her respect for ideas and information, but I think she was motivated most strongly by a kind of love I understand, the caring that wants the beloved to flourish. In the photographic record of her time in New York City, Jacobs appears in neat shift dresses adorned with a string of beads, gazing wryly through her cat's-eye glasses at a world that somehow rejects that caring but must be made to change. Her motherly quality added to her brilliance and determination.

The early teens of the twenty-first century were a fruitful period for me. I think it was because my heart and mind were free from the hard labor of a bad marriage. The daily battle of hope and fear had ended. I had always resisted being described as an optimist, believing that the word stood for a certainty I could not accept, that things would get better. Who can know the future? But once I understood that optimism meant seeing possibility whether or not it would ever be realized, I embraced it.

For the previous thirty years, I had been on a self-guided study of cultural policy. I understood from my reading in the international annals of that field that what passed for study in U.S. universities was generally a meager thing, focused largely on funding for artists and organizations. Conventional discourse in academia and the larger field had the suffocating quality of a cargo cult. Advocates seemed content to repeat the same failed approach in the vain hope it would at last succeed. They had been persuaded that it was necessary to talk to legislators in economistic language. Consequently, their advocacy focused on weak points, such as stressing how arts funding had a multiplier effect, with theater-ticket buyers also paying to eat, drink, and park. True enough, but in no way a special attribute of arts expenditure, as people who go to a football game or karaoke night at their favorite bar have the same economic impact. Believing that public and private policymakers could not be reached by arguments grounded in the necessity of art to human society, its powers to console and connect, even the largest and best-funded advocacy organizations failed

to acknowledge that in the time they had been behaving like a cargo cult—beginning with Ronald Reagan's election in 1980—the real value of the National Endowment for the Arts' budget had declined by more than half.

I saw that the inadequacy of this approach wasn't something that could be fixed with a few tweaks. The whole frame was wrong. It had been built by people whose minds were colonized by an extremely narrow and seldom questioned view of the possible. If we could exit that mind-set, it was in our collective power to build a much stronger frame.

I gave many talks outlining a paradigm shift I hoped was taking place, from worshipping the gray edifices of "Datastan"—where value could only be counted, weighed, and measured—to "Storyland," where we all have our stories, where feelings, metaphors, and images add up to a larger and truer picture of lived reality. I encouraged everyone I spoke with to ask what it would be like to give art and culture their real worth as the crucible in which our shared values and visions were forged. I invited them to consider how much poorer we were as a people when we dismissed them as frills, luxuries, and irrelevancies.

There were many opportunities to act on this insight. In 2009, I was one of a group of organizers who took advantage of an invitation to the White House to propose, among other things, that cultural recovery had to be part of the national recovery newly elected President Obama endorsed and hoped to fund. Central to our vision was a new public service employment program like the Works Progress Administration (WPA) of the 1930s New Deal or the 1970s Comprehensive Employment and Training Act (CETA) to put artists and others to work for the common good. We were ignored by the powers that be, but we did have some impact on enlarging the national conversation.

Every time I spoke, I asked three questions: Who are we as a people? What do we stand for? How do we want to be remembered?

I saw two ways to answer the last question. One was to earn the right to be seen for our vast creativity, for the daily kindnesses that greatly outnumber cruelties, and for the hope I cherished, that seeing how far we had strayed from a just, loving, and humane social order, we would act to put things right. The other came true when Trump was elected and our identity as the world's biggest punisher was sealed.

When I began to paint Jacobs, I discovered that there were many color images of her online in the last decades of her life, looking more and more gnomelike as she aged. I wanted to depict her around the time of her first book, but all of those images were black-and-white ones. I was mesmerized by a photo of a very young Jacobs at her typewriter, her glossy hair pulled back from a remarkable profile, as if all the energy of her formidable mind propelled her nose forward, leaving very little in the way of chin. But I needed to paint Jacobs in her forties. A kind friend connected

me with her son Jim, who was generous in explaining that "Jane had blue eyes that gradually got greyer as she got older. When I was a boy her hair was auburn." Auburn! Who would have thought?

I love Jacobs's keen eye for absurdity and her big heart, the empathy that fueled her successful fight to save her beloved Greenwich Village from planners' heartless determination to turn New York City into a place more suited for automobiles than human beings. I loved her courage in calling things as she saw them, as in *Dark Age Ahead,* her prescient 2004 book: "Credentialing, not educating, has become the primary business of North American universities." Hers was the clear vision that helped me understand the attitudes and entitlements that feed injustice, fueling the indifference of the few to the fate of the many. Today, half of the members of Congress are millionaires, insulated from citizens' common economic worries, and, to an alarming degree, evidently happy to leave the rest of us to our fate. This is a principal crisis of our society, one I fear may be permanent without many more voices like Jacobs's ringing out in every sphere, using ordinary language and everyday examples to connect us to the great questions that cannot be solved without us.

From Jane Jacobs, I understood that I could be exactly myself, ground-level affections and lofty ideals, that I could simply show up with all I had to offer. From Jane Jacobs, I took heart.

12

The Angels Confer

It wasn't until all eleven portraits were hanging in my studio and I sat down to start a new series of paintings that I decided to engage my angels in conversation. The room is long and narrow. The angel portraits hang on both long walls, arranged in chronological order to match the essays. They face one another over my easel and the table holding paint tubes, brushes, mediums, and other tools of the trade.

There are so many differences among the angels: when they lived and where, their genders, heritages, perspectives, relationships, accomplishments, and much more. It occurred to me to ask a new question: "What unites you?"

Many spoke at once, surprising me with the repetition of a single word: *exile.*

"From my country," said Paulo Freire, "after the 1964 coup."

"From my country," said Isaiah Berlin, "after the revolution."

"From my country," said Jane Jacobs, "after Moses had me arrested and the Vietnam War began."

"From this country," said Nina Simone, "which never deserved me."

"From this country," said James Baldwin, "which never understood love."

"From America," said John Trudell, "from the predator spirit mining our essence and our minds."

"From Europe," said Abraham Joshua Heschel; "I never returned. Every stone, every tree would remind me of children killed, of mothers burned alive, of human beings asphyxiated."

"From my family," said Doris Lessing.

"From my nature," Paul Goodman said.

"From my body," said Toulouse-Lautrec.

"From the art world," Alice Neel said, "but they took me back."

"Thank you," I told them. "I see that now. Everything you taught me requires the eyes of an outsider. You have to be able to discern the true nature of whatever others have normalized. The fish out of water sees so much more than his jauntily swimming sibling."

"Yes," said Paul Goodman. "But if it were only alienation, we could have stayed in our hiding places. We all had chutzpah, even when no one wanted to hear about it. Can I quote myself?"

"If we all can do the same," said Baldwin.

"This was published in 1962, friends," said Goodman. "'The present crisis in which an American writes is a peculiar one. He confronts in his audience the attitude that things are well enough, there is nothing to be grievous or angry about, and anyway our situation is inevitable. This attitude is the audience's technological and organizational helplessness mollified by the famously high standard of living. It puts a writer in the position of, as we Jews say, banging a teakettle, when his readers couldn't care less.'"

"*Hak mir nisht keyn tschaynik!*" I laughed. "My grandmother used to say that to me all the time: 'Don't bang a teakettle at me! Stop bothering me with your noise!'"

"Not just noise. Not just chutzpah," said Heschel. "Holy chutzpah, what Rebbe Nachman called *azut d'kedusha*. I translated it as 'spiritual audacity.' It's not easy to shut someone up who feels himself speaking for a higher purpose."

Baldwin looked at me. "You said I had it in your essay about me."

I smiled, so happy he'd noticed.

"Holy or not," Freire said, "as I am getting to know you all, I see we had it, the desire to stand up and speak truth despite the cost."

Know you all? Had they been talking when I wasn't around?

"There was so much bullshit," said Alice Neel, "it was like wading through mud. I felt I would be dragged down if I stopped to rest. Still, I wasn't about to let them stop me."

Lessing and Jacobs both nodded. "Let's not get into that ridiculous argument about truth," Lessing said. "There are many. But I have the idea that all of us sought it and tried to speak it when we succeeded."

There were lots of assenting sounds before Simone spoke up: "I may not be the only one who was accused of telling too much truth."

"Yes," said Baldwin, "I venture we were all charged with that crime."

Berlin chuckled. "I'll just say I was never accused of reticence."

Trudell rubbed his forehead. "But it wasn't me-me-me. There were so many people whose voices hadn't been heard. I was part of trying to break a long, deep silence."

"But silence was a two-way street: Some couldn't say the words; some couldn't hear them," said Freire.

"Amen," Baldwin said.

"Don't lose sight," Simone said; "for every one trying to silence us, a dozen wanted more."

"Sometimes," said Toulouse-Lautrec, "it wasn't words, but images, that wouldn't release us until we'd expressed them."

"Or music," said Trudell. "But none of us could keep silent about what we saw."

More than half my angels had chosen the path of art. I'd never counted before.

"Each time I sat in a circle with people discovering their subjectivity, their power to make the world, I felt I was witnessing a birth," Freire said.

"The birth of freedom," said Simone.

"Quoting myself seems a bit gauche," Berlin said, pointedly not looking at Goodman. "But we must remember that 'Freedom for the wolves has often meant death to the sheep.'"

"Give us this, though" Goodman said; "none of us was on the side of the predators. Where we got the ache that put us on the side of the suffering must take many different stories to tell, but we all had it. We felt it."

The studio filled with sounds of agreement, then with silence.

Exile and otherness, holy audacity, freedom, empathy, art—these sustain the Camp of Angels of Freedom. In fear and hope, the angels of freedom sustain our world.

PART TWO

What Does It Mean

to Be Educated?

My Agenda

I have an agenda in writing this book. I want us to prevent and heal the damage that credentialism—the certainty that academic qualifications are the best measure of ability—does to many people who lack college degrees. I speak for openness, awareness, and respect. I don't want to see human potential wasted, skill and knowledge squandered, people who have a great deal to contribute overlooked and devalued because they haven't been certified by an institution. I want to see the institutions that benefit from treating knowledge as their sole province held to account and reformed, especially those heaping up vast fortunes by making access ever scarcer and more expensive. I want all people to be granted the same freedom to pursue their chosen paths to knowledge and to be respected for their skill and wisdom whether or not they were acquired in an educational institution.

Yet when I talk about being an autodidact, I am sometimes treated like an irresponsible—even malevolent—force by people who fear I am trying to persuade others to reject formal education. The implication is that I was somehow uniquely qualified for this path, while talking positively about it would lead others astray. The archetypal other these individuals have in mind is a young person of color without economic advantage, someone they fear will face far greater obstacles than were put in my path if formal credentials are lacking.

They may not agree with my perspectives on education, but their concern reveals that they share my awareness of credentialism and its negative impacts. They may be right to fear—obviously so if the young person they have in mind wishes to enter a field in which credentials are a hard-and-fast prerequisite. It's also true that if academia is to be made more welcoming and reflective of the society at large, more graduates from marginalized groups must join faculties. I respect and support those who, believing in equity and justice, choose a path to the groves of academe. Formal higher education should be accessible to all who wish it.

But to those critics, let me be clear: I have absolutely no interest in recruiting autodidacts. Some people enter that category for reasons beyond their control. But for those who have a choice and are willing to live with its consequences, such decisions must be fully considered and uncoerced.

Nor is lifelong learning my subject. Just about everyone is self-taught to some degree. People commonly teach themselves to cook or knit, play the guitar, or speak another language without benefit of classroom instruction or certification. Lifelong learning is admirable. But I'm happy to leave advocating it to the many individuals and organizations already involved.

I support the freedom to choose one's own education. That freedom cannot be fully realized with social expectations or exclusionary gatekeepers blocking the way. Still, more people are making diverse choices. Among many such groups, for example, there's a fairly robust Black home-schooling and "unschooling" network created by parents who don't want to subject their children to the pernicious ideas and wounding experiences that are all too typical in classrooms. They evidently feel able to equip their children to make their own ways along the path of curiosity, need, and desire. Surely that is their right.

Especially in today's high-tech world, some people are strong advocates for unschooling. For instance, the right-wing-libertarian tech entrepreneur Peter Thiel established a sought-after fellowship for recipients who agree to drop out of college. Here's the motto: "The Thiel Fellowship gives $100,000 to young people who want to build new things instead of sitting in a classroom." The fellowship cohort has become a kind of elite network for ambitious and talented entrepreneurs whose gifts are judged by the work they do rather than by the degrees they've earned.

Both these examples are still exceptions to what's understood as normal. Both approaches are more likely to be attacked and defended than accepted. Anti-Blackness is undeniable, but some people act as if it cancels choice, prescribing graduate school as the only effective inoculation against a life of extreme deprivation. White skin privilege is undeniable, allowing me to drive without being pulled over by police, to enter buildings without being surveilled, and much more. But it doesn't automatically give me wealthy forebears or open doors to social power, even though some people behave as if it does. You can't glance at me and assume you know my reality, any more than I can presume to know yours based on a few outward characteristics. Yet many assertions about higher education do exactly that, attempting to foreclose people's choices "for their own good."

Beyond pointing out the damage done by credentialism and advocating respect for autodidacts, I have another aim in writing this book. I want to encourage the type of thinking about education that I happily prescribe as necessary in all spheres: penetrating analysis of what is, both its strengths and weaknesses; and propositional thinking, rich with both personal and social imagination about what could be.

Two ideas that are foundational to that intention struck me in the spring of 2022, when I offered a keynote address at a national conference of community-based artists and designers. I worked very hard on my text, driven by the sense that during

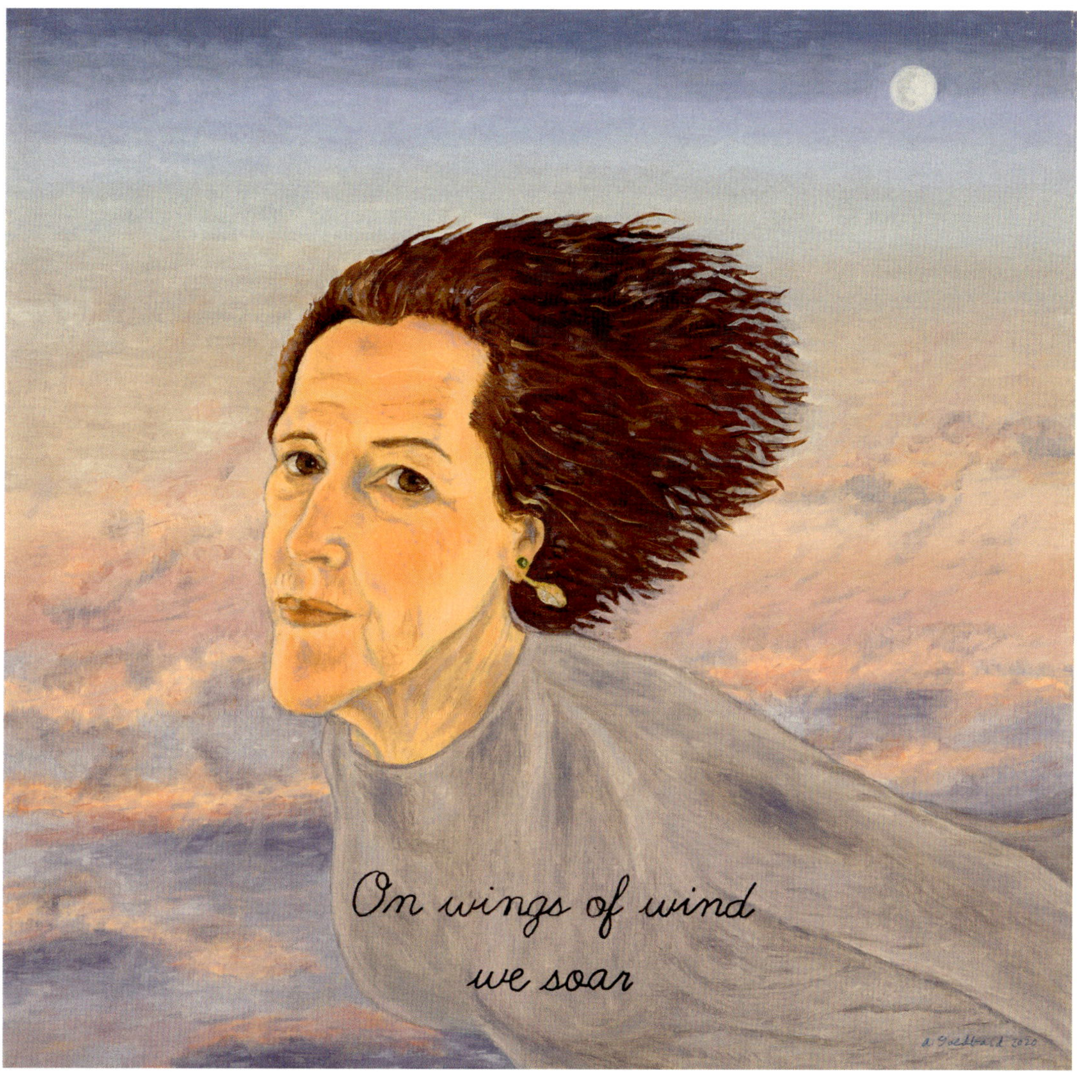

"On Wings of Wind," 24 x 24 inch oil on panel from the 2019 series, "Gaia and Shekhina Speak."

the previous two pandemic years, I'd found it difficult to think and easy to react. I doubted I was the only one, and wanted to offer something that could help reverse that.

I found my inspiration in the writing of Václav Havel, playwright and former Czech president, particularly his 1978 essay "The Power of the Powerless." It introduced me to two potent concepts. "Living within the lie" describes the countless daily submissions and gestures of compliance demanded by what Havel called the "post-totalitarian state." Even under such circumstances, by "living within the truth," ordinary people were able to choose everyday acts that honored and embodied their dignity. I made these the centerpiece of my talk, calling out some of the lies we are expected to live within and tracing the possible impact of what Havel called "the virus of truth [which] slowly spread through the tissue of the life of lies, gradually causing it to disintegrate." I would like to think I am helping that spread in some small way.

Dreams and Disparities

A friend of mine who read some of my writing on higher education—a retired professor, highly intelligent, well read, white, female, politically liberal—told me afterward that she had thoroughly enjoyed her college education, encountering few of the challenges that figure in my accounts. I should say that she went in the late sixties to one of the schools that had a national reputation for flexibility and experimentation (at that time, schools like Goddard, Antioch, Reed, and UC Santa Cruz), albeit largely white countercultural demographics (at my friend's undergraduate school, Black enrollment has never risen above the low single digits, for instance).

But even if she'd attended one of the most conventional schools or one of the most integrated and diverse, I would have no trouble believing her. It sounds dreamy to imagine years of reading, thinking, talking, writing, being introduced to new people and ideas, being challenged around the ones I know. I'm certain that had I chosen it, I could have had a truly enlarging and memorable higher education experience.

My times on college campuses have been confusing, though, taking the edge off that higher ed dream. I've encountered many gifted and dedicated educators and administrators, and admired their commitment and perseverance. All of them expressed frustration about the constraints their institutions impose. Many were convinced of the impossibility of challenging these restrictions, given academic hierarchy and the slowness with which institutions entertain change. Sometimes the challenges are macro: being part of a theater or visual arts school within a university where systems have been shaped to fit the largest student populations in business, science and technology, education, and so on, whose needs will be very different from studio-based arts education. Sometimes they are micro: the daunting paperwork to be filed and numerous gatekeepers to be satisfied in designing a new course or making it possible to coteach across departmental lines. The institutional barriers and stumbling blocks plaguing higher education need repair and revision. The frustrations are real, and by no means trivial.

Yet I admit that for someone like myself, working from project to project without the benefits and job security provided for tenured faculty, after listening to many complaints about the system, a little voice sounds. It wonders if a reality check might persuade tenured faculty to compare their own working conditions and compensation with those of people who never get a summer off or a sabbatical every seventh year, who wait tables or stand at an assembly line and fantasize about winning the lottery as an exit strategy.

I'm an outsider, but the same questions are asked by insiders. Tenured faculty make up an ever-smaller group in many colleges, with more and more teaching slots filled by adjunct professors and other part-timers (who lack not only job security but commensurate compensation and benefits). When they talk to me about their jobs, the stories are much grimmer.

Institutional blockages notwithstanding, there remains considerable flexibility in classrooms and studios, and I'm certain that many students who are the contemporary counterparts of my friend have an experience just as stimulating and worthwhile as she did in the sixties.

But the story isn't the same for everyone. Only 40 percent of Black students graduate within six years of enrolling, in contrast to 64 percent of white students.[1] In every school I've visited, there are faculty members who believe strongly that their color, gender, or sexual orientation carries a responsibility to reach out and support students who know what it is to feel other. They have experienced the challenges firsthand and often derive considerable satisfaction from helping to address them. They invest tremendous effort in keeping students in school despite taxing home lives and precarious resources.

The differentials in access and success for different groups of college students are major and serious. Despite the existence of programs intended to reduce them, they are not being addressed with the energy and rigor they ought to demand, and this is being noticed. In January 2022, for instance, a lawsuit by former students accused a consortium of sixteen prestigious colleges of overcharging some 170,000 students over the last twenty years, hiding behind an exemption from antitrust law that was intended to enable them to collaborate in fairly assessing students' financial need.[2] The exemption was supposed to ensure that the institutions didn't compete in offering financial aid, but instead, all used the same formula. The suit charged that in reality, it resulted in significantly less financial aid being granted than at schools outside the consortium, depriving students of needed support and channeling the funds not offered to students into institutional priorities having nothing to do with access and equity.

The grip of credentialism, racism, and elitism is strong. More and more, it is normalized. The disrespect meted out to those without higher education credentials is rooted in the fantasy that academia is a meritocracy with a deserved monopoly on learning. Many people who have nothing to gain by supporting a social order based on class culling by educational and social institutions nevertheless come to see this as normal, as just a fact of life.
If you went to college, I hope that your experience was as gratifying as my friend's. But individual experience doesn't in any way cure or cancel my reasons for writing this book: to urge respect for the self-educated, and to call out the forces that devalue them.

The Auto Club

More than a decade ago, I decided to write a very different book about self-education. I had a good title: "The Auto Club: Alternate Routes to Higher Education." I had a great many noteworthy names to cite. Some of them appeared in the first paragraph of the introductory essay:

In my great-grandparents' time, almost everyone belonged. Today, zillionaire

Microsoft founder Bill Gates and his partner Paul Allen are card-carrying members, as are rivals Larry Ellison of Oracle and the two Steves (Jobs and Wozniak) of Apple. They join the illustrious ranks of James Baldwin, Ray Bradbury, C. L. R. James, Doris Lessing, Stanley Kubrick, Woody Allen, Richard Wright, Claire Booth Luce, David Ben-Gurion, Richard Avedon, Frank Zappa, Agatha Christie, Gore Vidal, Walt Disney, William Faulkner, Emma Goldman, and Hazel Henderson. Oh, and did I mention Ansel Adams, J. D. Salinger, George Bernard Shaw, August Wilson, Eleanor Roosevelt, Orson Welles, and Steven Spielberg?

(If I were writing this today, my list of "auto club" members would be much longer, including Jorge Luis Borges, Eugene O'Neill, August Wilson, Noël Coward, Booker T. Washington, Bruce Springsteen, Frank Lloyd Wright, Thomas Alva Edison, Buckminster Fuller, Jane Jacobs, Karl Marx, Frederick Douglass, Susan B. Anthony, Sojourner Truth, Mary Wollstonecraft, Fannie Lou Hamer, Lenny Bruce, Ida B. Wells, Cesar Chavez, Fran Leibowitz, Frida Kahlo, Malcolm X, and a raft of others.)

It seemed like a good time for such a book, as entrepreneurs and original thinkers were gaining visibility as autodidacts. In the high-tech world in particular, there was growing acceptance that formal education could not train students for roles that had not yet been invented. Indeed, the requisite qualities for success—imagination, creativity, resourcefulness, open-mindedness, and so on—seldom originated in the classroom.

My intention, threaded through nearly everything I've written that touches on questions of social status and privilege, was to draw attention to the vast human potential of the unschooled—shamefully disregarded and disrespected—and to point out the power of self-education, which can lead to discoveries unconstrained by the systems that legitimate some types of knowledge and devalue others.

My thought was that profiling successful and accomplished autodidacts would illuminate the unrecognized potential of those whose success stories had been thwarted by credentialism. I interviewed a couple of notable autodidacts and wrote their stories as sample chapters accompanying the book proposal I sent to agents. The second time an agent rejected the project but asked if it would be okay to keep the proposal as a well-written exemplar to share with other writers, I began to give up on the idea. What finally convinced me was the response from an agent who said she'd enjoyed the proposal but thought I'd have much more of a platform from which to pursue the subject if I had a Ph.D.!

13

The Education of an Autodidact

The Lessons of the Porcelain Room

The Porcelain Room was a forest of sparkling vitrines, each displaying ceramic objects organized by European historical period: ancient Roman here, majolica there, early porcelain objects elsewhere. They filled a large airy space that opened onto the de Young Museum's garden in San Francisco's Golden Gate Park.

I liked visiting museums, even though entering one usually prompted me to hold my breath and walk on tiptoe. This was the mid-seventies, so I hadn't yet read Pierre Bourdieu's research concerning what ordinary French people felt museums were most like, but I knew the answer from my own body's response: *churches,* of course, aspirational spaces demanding best behavior. On that day, though, I hadn't gone there to admire the porcelain, but to meet with the trustees of the Fine Arts Museums of San Francisco. I was nervous as I threaded my way past the glass cases, searching for the table and chairs set out for our meeting.

The surroundings spoke of preciousness and fragility, and I felt out of place.

I was an organizer for a group called the San Francisco Art Workers' Coalition. We were performers, visual artists, writers, and more, with very different practices: muralists, circus clowns, commedia actors, musicians, poets, media makers. What we had in common were certain democratic, liberatory values. Our work gave us an insider's view of what are conventionally called "the arts," a term I dislike for its clumsy grouping of big-ticket, red-carpet institutions with tiny, beleaguered, insurgent groups. While from the outside, the world of theaters, galleries, and so on may look like a chummy and well-funded enclave of privilege, sweetness, and light, from the inside, the economics (and thus the power relations) are nearly feudal, with fat-cat organizations hoovering up most of the resources and everyone else scrambling for the leftovers.

We believed this should change. Since the Fine Arts Museums were publicly owned and funded in part with taxpayers' dollars, we thought they should be accountable to all communities in the city they were chartered to serve. That translated into many ideas, such as making room on their self-perpetuating governing boards for artists and other community members more committed to equity and far less involved with the city's social and economic elites, and showing the work of women and artists of color, including living artists.

To back up our claims, we'd done a great deal of research, plotting the trustees' interlocking financial and social interests on a map, generating a thick tangle of red lines that looked like the plan for a new freeway between the ritzy Pacific Heights neighborhood and the Financial District.

In the lead-up to the bicentennial of the American Revolution in 1976, the de Young Museum was planning a celebratory exhibition of John D. Rockefeller III's collection of American art, later bequeathed to the museum to form the nucleus of its American Wing. We found the exhibition and timing objectionable in multiple ways. The collection comprised almost entirely art by white men—I recall there was one painting by a woman and none by a person of color, but maybe it was the other way around. This seemed especially egregious, as it was the only exhibit any local museum planned for the occasion, and it telegraphed the message that this country was made by white men, that their perceptions, subjects, and depictions told the definitive story for us all.

We were also aware of the means whereby the market system adds value to art objects. When JDR III began to acquire this work, American painting was not much in demand. Today the museum highlights recognizable American Wing names and images on its website—Copley, Homer, Church. But when most of the collection was purchased, pieces were generally obscure and often obtained for a fraction of the value that quickly accrued *because* they were first exhibited at and then acquired by a major museum. What was being billed solely as an act of generosity was also a shrewd financial stratagem.

I was a spokesperson for our group, assigned that day to represent our demands for accountability for taxpayers' funding, inclusive and equitable exhibition policies, and meaningful representation for all San Franciscans in the museums' governance. The meeting unfolded pretty much as expected. We spoke, the trustees offered a few questions and comments, but nothing was explicitly agreed or rejected. We felt they were waiting for us to be gone to get on with their real business. Soon we were making our way past the vitrines toward the exit.

Before we left the building, a curator took me aside. Genial, graying, he peered at me over his gold-rimmed glasses, leaning in to speak in a softly confiding voice. "The trustees would be fine with adding someone like you," he whispered, "someone who understands. Didn't you go to one of the Seven Sisters?"

I'd never heard that name before. I had to visit the library to learn that it referred to seven historic northeastern women's colleges: Mount Holyoke, Smith, Wellesley, Bryn Mawr, Barnard, Vassar, and Radcliffe.

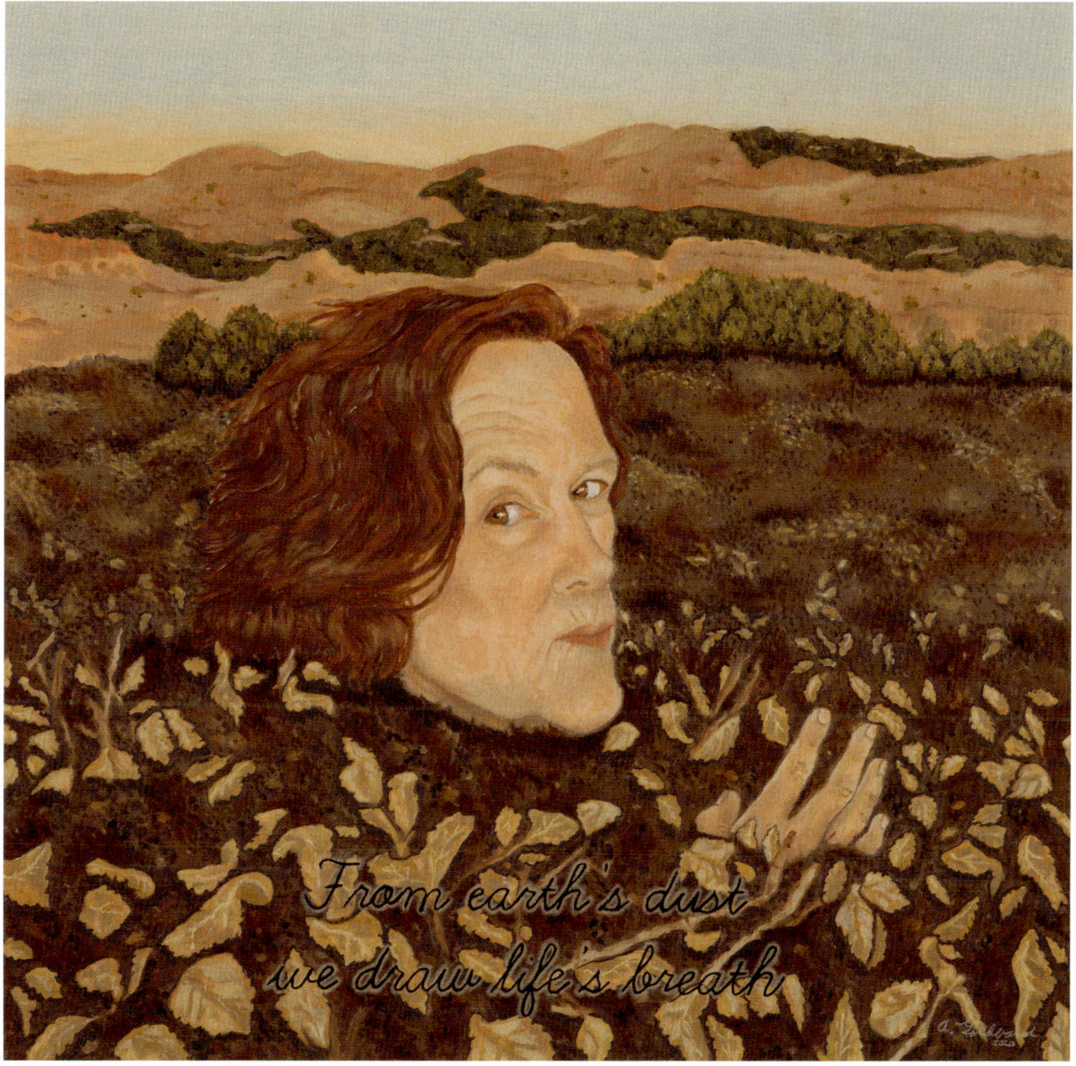

"From Earth's Dust," 24 x 24 inch oil on panel from the 2019 series, "Gaia and Shekhina Speak."

This memory stands out vividly because it so fully encapsulates several things I want to say about education.

There is a persuasive and widespread official story situating formal higher education as the sole source of valid knowledge. It is commonly accepted, and not only by those schooled at colleges and universities.

Yet is perfectly possible to educate oneself such that an observer cannot distinguish an autodidact from someone fully credentialed via formal higher education.

Many people with social and economic privilege perceive certain qualities—articulateness, intelligence, intellectual confidence—as attributes of privilege resembling their own, blithely assuming they've been acquired at what they consider first-rate schools. How else?

For those aligned with these perceptions, having obtained a degree from such a school confers a sense of fellowship and shared value, regardless of how long ago it happened. The trustees imagined a comfortable backstory for me, believing that what I'd supposedly done for a few years in my youth had legitimated me forever after.

Those sharing such views require indicators of privilege as the price of a ticket to polite society. The trustees were okay with inviting someone perceived as "one of us" onto the board; they were not okay with inviting someone who would disrupt their comfortable assumptions of belonging.

Therefore, a sense of safety or security is embedded in these beliefs: The trustees felt comfortable with me because my manner and conduct reassured them that although I was critical, I would be safe to bring inside the citadel. They thought they could trust me to maintain decorum.

I had no way of knowing whether the invitation to join the trustees was sincere or merely a way of testing whether my self-interest trumped public interest. It was never repeated and I never pursued it. But if I had, and if I had also identified myself as an autodidact, class-conscious, and far less interested in decorum than truth, I am certain the invitation would have been withdrawn—or more likely, quietly allowed

to drop. Since I lacked the credentials that would have augmented the museum's prestige, I would have been recognized as an outsider and treated accordingly.

Together, these attitudes add up to a way of looking at the world and its people that squanders the lived knowledge and intelligence of vast numbers for whom being educated means pursuing their own curiosity and honing their own skills, people indifferent or hostile to the rituals of social status among the privileged.

All of us have the capacity to interrogate our own assumptions if only we also have the desire to do so. The question of what it means to be educated is encrusted with untested assumptions. My hope is that readers will want to scrutinize them.

This chapter turns on my own education, the parts that came to me outside the classroom as much as those that took place in school. It also includes experiences with people who glorify formal higher education or denigrate self-education. I want to illuminate not only what I've learned and how but also the ways that social attitudes can deform perception of uncredentialed knowledge, harming those who have much to contribute despite their lack of degrees.

Junior High

As a child in school, I knew I was smart. I tended to have the answers when the teacher asked. I made it all the way to the last round of the school district's spelling bee. I got good grades without really trying. I scored high on standardized tests, which felt like some type of validation. But it came with a double edge.

In seventh grade, my first year in junior high school, an IQ test was administered to all students. Some memories of that time and place are still vivid. I can see the mission-style campus, the tile roofs and stucco walls, the shortcut we took to school through waste ground and eucalyptus groves. I can see the seventh-grade building, a one-story rectangle off to one side. Instead of staying with the same teacher throughout the school day, as we'd done in elementary school, all of us rotated through four different classrooms. That felt very grown-up.

I can see my classroom, three solid walls and one made of windows. I'm sitting, typically bored, perhaps three rows from the front, somewhere in the middle of the room. The teacher is a man—I hadn't had male teachers till that year. His name is long gone, but the mental image persists: early middle age, pleasant rather than handsome, shades of beige and brown, and an emphatic way of talking that must have been intended to awaken us from our collective stupor of hormones and self-consciousness.

The teacher tells the class that the test results have come in. He asks the students to guess who got the highest score. People call out the names of the boys everyone knows as "brains." Most of them wear thick glasses, carry slide rules in their shirt pockets, belong to clubs I know nothing about, blush if noticed. "No," says the teacher after each name, smiling and shaking his head. "Try harder." At last he tells us who scored highest. "Goldbard!" he exclaims, grinning. Some classmates are skeptical. Some just look at me in amazement. I know the teacher is trying to show what a mistake it is to underestimate people. But the way he has done it, staging a display that contrasts the me everyone sees with the me who took the test, merely confirms my otherness. I want to sink into the floor.

My memory of those days is highly imperfect. I see a few bright moments, a few embarrassing ones. The rest have faded. So I may be wrong, but I can't recall any member of the faculty or staff approaching me after that day, perhaps offering some learning opportunity to lighten the boredom I felt at the standard curriculum. I don't think I told anyone at home what had happened. But I've never forgotten it.

High School

It's been a long time since I was in school, but I still remember many of the subtle (and not so subtle) mechanisms used to separate students deemed worthy of excelling from the rest.

As a high school freshman, I was slotted into an English course designed mostly to occupy rambunctious students for an hour before they were released into the hallways for a quick discharge of suppressed energies. A typical learning experience would be a pop quiz on *Moby-Dick*: How many kinds of whales appear in the book? Why are they hunted? Who is Queequeg? My sympathetic counselor—like me, the child of working-class Jewish immigrants—noticed my stupefaction and transferred me to an advanced class featuring actual discussions. If he hadn't been there, I'm quite sure I would have slept through all four years of English.

I loved him for his willingness to see human potential regardless of the way it was packaged, for his spirit, which loved learning and wished that love to suffuse the world.

I am grateful I was assigned a counselor who cared and understood. The faculty as a whole—just as with the faculties I have since come across on my visits to college campuses—seemed exactly like the people one finds everywhere. Some were present and curious and determined; some were just serving time and not much bothered by the effect that had on those they taught.

At all educational levels, most faculty members I've encountered have been critical of the institutional culture in which their work is embedded. But few have said they feel responsible for it or able to change it, often accepting that the salient decisions were made long ago and above their pay grade. In our conversations, many have regarded institutional values and culture as given, a landscape independent of—and indifferent to—themselves.

This is understandable: Bureaucracy is stubborn. Who wants to bang their heads against the wall? But deferential acceptance of things as they are fosters insensitivity to what sociologists Richard Sennett and Jonathan Cobb called "the hidden injuries of class." If adapting to a system is regarded as the path to success, then those who can't or won't fully adapt will easily come to be seen as deficient. To some, such students need to fix their adjustment problems; to me, they ought to be understood as harbingers of necessary institutional change.

A classic focus-group exercise used to explain how issues are framed shows a picture of sick cattle in a field. Focus-group members are asked how the animals got that way. Usually, respondents say that the farmer failed to supply the animals with healthy food, or that they'd contracted a virus. (*Students lack diligence or ambition or discipline.*) Then the picture is enlarged to show a factory just beyond the farm, belching black smoke and effluent. Suddenly, larger answers emerge. (*Credentialism, elitism, and racism distort students' experience.*)

My high school counselor singled me out for a more stimulating round of classes than were prescribed for students no one saw as exceptions. That was fortunate for me. But where were the faculty members and counselors advocating for a more dynamic, engaging, challenging curriculum for all students? In the intervening decades, the opposite has too often been allowed to happen: teaching to standardized tests and spending more and more time in what my angel Paulo Freire called "banking education"—depositing rote information like coins into a piggybank—which often means sitting at a computer ticking multiple-choice boxes. When intervening to improve the culture of actually existing schools doesn't seem realistic to a significant number of faculty members and students, how can the system be changed? Any meaningful attempt to answer that question must show not just a close-up of the field—the classroom—but the whole scene that sustains a class system, polluting factory and all.

Disposition and Choice

It may be temperament or history or happenstance that propels someone onto the autodidact's path. Here's the story I often tell: I postponed going to college for a year after high school graduation to get married and support my husband in completing his degree in journalism. Once having lived as an adult, I then found Cooper Union, the school to which I'd been accepted, too much like high school: ringing bells, a limited curriculum, too many rules and not enough options. Perhaps if I'd landed in a more wide-open educational environment, I would have wanted to stay.

That story is true as far as it goes, but also I'd been stupid to marry at seventeen, picked the wrong man, found myself desperately lonely and unhappy in our little Brooklyn Heights apartment. I watched the *Million Dollar Movie* every day even though they screened the same picture daily for a whole week. In my memory it was always *The Bride of Frankenstein*. No place welcomed me, and I couldn't summon the heart to make a place for myself where I'd landed. I had to be on my own.

That's a true story, too, but I think the essentially autodidactic character of my personality may offer the deepest truth. I always liked to figure things out for myself. I don't mind guidance and often ask for advice, but in a situation where one is expected to follow the leader at the leader's pace, I usually want out. I notice this all the time: My friends who study yoga or Pilates look for a class; I look for a video or a book. Before I surrendered to the reality of my own nature, I put myself in the way of group instruction many times, and almost always put myself right out again.

When Prejudice Shows

By now I have lived a long life as a visual artist, writer, adviser, speaker, activist, and more, publishing books and essays, showing up in media interviews, speaking at universities and professional gatherings. No credentials, degrees, certificates, licenses. I wish I could embed a video clip in this page to show you the expression of astonishment on the faces of friends and colleagues upon learning this. Every time I see it, I think the same thing: You are looking at me as if I were a dog or a rabbit that suddenly stood on its hind legs and declaimed. Your prejudice is showing. They believe that what I did for four years—or six, or eight—more than fifty years ago makes a great difference in who I am now. And to anyone who has truly internalized the dominant idea of higher education as a necessary marker of legitimacy, as having monopolized learning, it does. It does.

Some surprising people partake of this prejudice, automatically characterizing autodidacts as marginalized by their status. As I was finishing this book, an acquaintance—a writer strongly identified with social justice issues—put out a call for self-taught visual artists. I responded. He told me he hadn't made this explicit in his request, but the two artists he'd thus far found were "long-term houseless, so just by virtue of your success you're not quite . . . what I'm looking for."

Very little of the learning that enabled me to become myself took place in educational settings. Instead, the knowledge I've found most useful was imparted outside the classroom, first through observation—chiefly, staring for hours at the drawings and paintings of artists whose work spoke to me, even if the connection sometimes seemed unfathomable to others. Second, my knowledge has come through books I was lucky enough to pick up when it was most necessary for me to read them. When the student is ready, they say, the teacher will arrive. And third, I have learned through direct transmission, through tender hearts and sharp minds generously willing to share what they knew.

The Power of a Knack

Curiosity and desire motivate the autodidact, but where do they come from? For me, it's usually discovering a knack.

For example, an ongoing part of my work has been facilitating meetings. The facilitator is that neutral party who leads the dialogue, recognizing the next speaker, summing up, intervening to move things along. Beginning in the sixties, I plunged into forms of activism and organizing that required many meetings—working with young men subject to the military draft or demonstrating against the Vietnam War, engaging with groups of artists who wanted to change cultural policy or funding patterns, becoming involved in progressive Jewish community, and more. I have taken part in thousands of meetings.

I found the typical countercultural meeting of the sixties and seventies frustrating. By the time all those in the circle had checked in, describing their moods, concerns, adventures (and astrological signs), two-thirds of the meeting time was gone, and the balance could be disposed of via an argument over trivialities treated as if the world depended on the outcome.

I wish I had captured some of the epic battles over things like the color of paper for a flyer, each side of the debate heaping symbolic or political meanings onto the question at hand until it resembled, in Bob Dylan's description, a mattress balanced on a bottle of wine.

This wasn't just a sixties countercultural phenomenon. It pervaded much of second-wave feminism. Similar patterns emerged in Occupy Wall Street groups. The absence of designated authority or any formal process for advancing people to some type of leadership creates a power vacuum easily filled by anyone given to self-promotion and not overly concerned about equity. Saying "There are no leaders here" inevitably invites someone to step up and say "Follow me!" I'm allergic to that.

Growing up in my family prepared me to be a facilitator. I can't remember a time in my childhood when I didn't look around the house and say to myself, These people are nuts. Somebody'd better be thinking here; I guess it will have to be me.

Throwing myself into vibrant cultural and political movements triggered some of the feelings I'd had in dealing with my family: These people need help to talk with one another in a respectful and productive way! At first I offered interventions that could clarify something or make space for possibility. Later I suggested ways of organizing the agenda and discussion that could help people accomplish the work rather than becoming mired in process. After that, people started asking me to lead meetings. Then they hired me to plan and facilitate them. Fast forward fifty years and I admit that it's hard for me to sit through a meeting I'm not facilitating, unless the person who is takes a similar approach.

I've been thinking about my self-directed way of learning to facilitate meetings, how much it contrasts with formal facilitator-training opportunities, which are pretty thick on the ground. Many are branded approaches, often offering some type of certification. Most are technique-heavy, teaching tactics for small-group work or ways to get out of stuck situations, proposing ideas for icebreakers and offering note-taking tips.

But here's the thing: I don't think the essential qualities of presence, deep listening, and love can be taught. If you aren't torqued that way—if it doesn't give you pleasure to see someone you don't particularly like rise in fullness to meet a moment;

if despite a healthy ego, you don't feel wonderful when you are able to entirely ignore your own opinions when they don't really matter—you are unlikely to have the necessary qualifications. But if those essential qualities are intrinsic to your nature, then study and practice can only improve them.

How many skills are similar? How many are seeded by a knack that is more essential to mastery than any amount of formal training? Most important, can this type of skill be recognized, acknowledged, and given its rightful place among the stock of abilities a decent society needs? I was able to do this work because colleagues and clients recommended me to others. So that's a partial answer: An informal network grounded in direct experience can give value to something uncredentialed, something outside the formal disciplines that populate higher education. But that still leaves many people facilitating meetings who don't bring the necessary depth, flexibility, and knowledge but whose credentials carry them forward, heedless of the damage they may do.

Imagine the society that allows—encourages—people to discover their knacks organically, through observation of their own experience, and helps us all to develop them through practice and reflection. That's where I want to live.

What Does It Mean to Be Educated?

Given so many routes to knowledge, the variety of personal opportunities and proclivities, what does it mean to be educated?

To me, it means having engaged with the collective stock of human knowledge sufficient to develop awareness of self, others, and environment; cognitive skills; critical thinking; problem-solving ability; social and personal imagination; recognition of one's own and others' emotions and the capability to respond with sensitivity and compassion; capacity to communicate to the best of one's ability; and, above all else, curiosity to always seek further knowledge. Knowledge itself may be experiential, practical, or discovered through reading and other forms of recording and communication. I see no hierarchy here.

As a veteran and admirer of self-education, my answer is independent of institutions. I am one of legions who—whether by virtue of class, immigration, religion, race, or any category society assigns us in the hope that knowing our places, we will remain in them—have taught ourselves to comprehend the customs and mores of our time. I can perform the codes and gestures that make privileged people comfortable with the tacit assumption that I am one of them. I also know how to shake them out of that presumption.

Many people emerge from formal education with some of the capabilities I've listed; many do not. I've met virtuoso scholars whose mastery of their subjects knocked me off my feet and Ph.D. candidates who found writing a simple business letter beyond their skill set—and beneath them to boot. In the mid-seventies, I was asked by the California Arts Council, a state agency, to create a service that provided information, training, and grants to artists and groups. To augment the small staff, we were helped by student interns from the University of California at Davis, not far from our office in Sacramento. I gave one intern the assignment of answering queries. Back then, actual letters on paper had to be typed and posted.

After his first day on the job, the intern brought me a couple of his finished letters to review. Each consisted of a single sentence summarizing the requested information—for instance, "Here is the document you wanted." I explained that business letters needed to be cordial, since part of our task was cultivating working relationships: "Thank you for writing"; "We're happy to let you know we can provide that information"; "Please don't hesitate to contact us if you have further questions"; and so on. (I realize that in the age of email and text, many people dispense with all that, but take it from me, it was standard practice.)

The intern was remarkably upset about this. "You want me to write massage-parlor letters!" he accused. I asked if he'd ever written this type of letter before. The answer was no. His fields of study were drama and creative writing.

This is merely an anecdote, obviously. But over time and many not-for-profit projects, I discovered essentially the same thing, that most student interns from comfortable and protected households possessed very little practical knowledge. The sense I got was that it hadn't occurred to them that they would need it. People had secretaries to write letters for them. Being educated meant obtaining a credential in their chosen field before moving into a way of life in which the tasks that others cannot escape are taken on by underlings employed for that purpose.

Today, when cultural assumptions that reinforce hierarchy and privilege are more closely scrutinized, greater numbers perceive the dynamics that have created different rules for working while female or driving while Black. But in a country in which something like 80 percent of those asked to place themselves on the socioeconomic ladder say middle-class (a mathematical impossibility and a neatly diabolical trick to erase class consciousness), some biases are seldom fully acknowledged. And in many educational systems, whether with conscious intent or through a kind of automatism, some biases are reproduced ad infinitum.

Where Love Is Inappropriate

In 2008, I took part in a research project to assess the current situation and future prospects for community-based artists in higher education. In the early 2000s, there was a little explosion of such programs. The nomenclature was anything but uniform: Among the degrees then granted were some in Community Arts, Applied Theater, Theater for Youth, Public Art, Directing and Public Dialogue, and so on. My colleagues and I surveyed hundreds of individuals and dozens of programs involved in this type of education. We produced a report, sharing our data and offering recommendations as to how the field could be strengthened.

The report was circulated in draft form to quite a few of the participants, as we wanted to be sure our account was accurate. We were delighted at the positive response. There were very few corrections or suggestions for revision—with one exception. A number of the faculty members surveyed objected to the text embedded in a small graphic that portrayed our approach to the subject. (See figure)

For our team, community engagement, training, and scholarship were the three pillars of "community cultural development in higher education," which was also the report's title. The quotation that appears in the center of the image is from the Reverend James Lawson, Jr., a founder of the 1960s Student Nonviolent Coordinating Committee (SNCC) and author of the guiding principles adopted by that civil rights organization. It articulated SNCC's aim, one we thought perfectly encapsulated a core goal of the kind of education we wrote about. We were making the point that the center of the work was not just mastering the three pillars but also clarity about the reasons to do so.

Those faculty members who objected said that the word *love* did not belong in a report dealing with higher education.

Some said it was inappropriate, others too open to interpretation, but whatever their reasons, the word made half a dozen of our respondents uncomfortable. That broke my heart and also shocked me: What did it mean for students that love did not belong in academic discourse?

We kept it in.

Higher Education and the Nirvana Fallacy

In my experience with higher education institutions, there has been far more emphasis on critique than possibility. Academics often make their bones by pointing out what's wrong, missing, problematic in their areas of study.

Take a pet interest of mine, the Works Progress Administration (WPA) of the 1930s, called into being by President Franklin Delano Roosevelt as part of public response to the Great Depression. Among many WPA initiatives that gave paying work to people who were formerly on relief, five arts programs grouped under the title "Federal One" supported visual artists, writers, performers, and others in offering their work for the public good. Because they left an enormous legacy of public art and design, arts programs often come first to mind when people think of the WPA. During the COVID-19 pandemic, with its disastrous economic impact, many people called for a revival of similar programs, and in 2021 and early 2022, some small initiatives along these lines came to pass, mostly supported by foundations.

The WPA wasn't perfect—what is? But it enabled some remarkable things: supporting Black theaters where none had existed, documenting nearly all the extant narratives of enslaved people, an index of American design, and much more. As an exemplar, it raises an important and ever-green question about the impact and necessity of public investment in social and cultural goods. There are several notable organizations and archives devoted to preserving and extending its legacy.

Find a database of academic papers about the WPA, though, and this story may have a different tilt. Many authors search for all they can fault—and there was plenty, given the thirties zeitgeist and mores, from gender and racial inequities to overbearing regional directors for whom free expression was better if not quite so free. The most critical papers have a certain uniformity: *You think this was great, hmm? Well, think again!* I venture that papers may achieve higher marks if they expose clay feet than if they celebrate something of value and point to ways that value can be revived. Very often, the convention is to pile up enough criticism to sink an idea. The cognitive scientists have something to say about this: The "Nirvana fallacy" is comparing some actually existing thing with an idealized version that can never be fully achieved in real life and, of course, finding it wanting. In these contexts, I see little awareness of the countervailing perspective expressed in Voltaire's maxim, one I have found worth living by: "The perfect is the enemy of the good."

Critical intelligence is a good thing if it's balanced by a propositional mind-set and social imagination. But the overemphasis on negativity in academia is problematic. It sometimes arises when I speak to college classes or at university symposia. A perpetual theme in my work is the notion of a culture of possibility. Many people are afraid to conceive a better future, afraid that getting their hopes up will only invite greater disappointment. The problem is that the alternative is a kind of resignation both pliant and cynical. Holding a conviction that power lies elsewhere and cannot be moved ends up ceding the future to the powers that be, whose addiction to the done thing means they aren't really qualified for the role.

In the interactive parts of my presentations, people who seem far too young to be so jaundiced commonly tell me that what I'm imagining is impossible to attain. They may turn out to be right; we can't know the future until it unfolds. But such judgments, often about vast systems and historic forces, cannot be grounded in direct knowledge or experience of a future yet to arrive. The question I find interesting is what has persuaded these young people to be so cynical and hopeless.

I'm not suggesting that this hopelessness is entirely the fault of academic institutions. Indeed, a frequent question I receive when I talk with college students is how to feel less demoralized. By now, I have an automatic response, which is to ask how much news the questioner consumes daily via the internet, social media, print, or broadcast media. Most conscientious young people seem to feel a great responsibility to keep up, so the answer is that they are perpetually plugged in. I mention what the

cognitive researchers call an "availability cascade," where something makes the news and is then picked up by other outlets and reflected back to still others, until the item in question expands to temporarily occupy the entire news sphere. Many of these news flashes are less than urgent or earthshaking, but because the media are hungry ghosts for novelty, they repeat and resound.

"If it bleeds, it leads." If we don't understand and correct for this addiction, we drown our awareness in a constant supply of freshly spilled blood. This dynamic distorts reality in disturbing ways. I recall reading the results of a massive social science experiment in which several similar questions were hidden in a long survey, thus producing more revealing answers than if they had been asked only once. One outcome was that people rated their chances of dying from a terrorist bombing as greater than their chances of dying in an explosion, even though the former is a subset of the latter.

This defies logic but not understanding. Headlines inflate terrorism's dangers, making the threat seem larger and more imminent than, say, an ordinary gas leak. The National Fire Protection Association estimates that about four thousand gas leak–related fires and forty deaths take place in the United States each year.[3] There were eight deaths from terrorism—all at the hands of domestic far-right perpetrators—in the United States in 2020, none of them from explosions.[4] There were no mass terrorist attacks in the United States in 2021.[5]

I do, however, hold educators responsible to teach students the awareness and skill needed not only to cultivate and exercise social imagination but to become critical consumers of information, to notice when their minds are being colonized, to reduce the dosage, to know when to take a break. I've encountered some very good professors who accept and execute this responsibility, but on the campuses I've visited, I've never heard anyone outside of media studies describe this as an essential mission.

I'm not a Pollyanna. I have no way of being certain whether or not the more democratic and humane society I envision will come about. I only know that if students are led to develop their critical capacities and fault-finding orientation to a point of being mentally musclebound, and if they have almost no training or encouragement in positive social imagination, the culture of impossibility takes hold, and that is a dangerous place to live.

When young people are headed to college, I want them to be prepared, to avoid succumbing to dominant attitudes that may dampen their sense of possibility, to avoid falling unawares into institutional customs that reinforce elitist ideas and false hierarchies of value. I want them to think about what it means to be educated, and not stop their thinking at improving job prospects. I want them to embark on their formal education and also come away from it with full respect for all types of knowledge, credentialed and lived, and for the people who acquire and possess them.

Is that too much to ask?

The Pedagogy of Cruelty

My personal preference has been for self-education because it allows the committed seeker of knowledge to range widely, exploring with equal curiosity ideas with solid slots in the canon and insurgent perspectives. In contrast, I've often seen educational institutions promote problematic ways of thinking and being, and, either by omission or outright condemnation, deprecate others.

Here's one story. Speaking engagements have been a major part of my work. Many invitations come from college arts departments. Typically, I'll spend a few days on campus giving a talk, offering workshops, speaking with classes, meeting with students and faculty, and so on. A common practice in visual arts programs is to invite visitors to engage in a few critique sessions with students who are often required to complete a number of such critiques. The hope is that they will benefit from the response to their work by knowledgeable people who are seeing it for the first time.

More than a decade ago, I was invited by visual arts faculty to a university where one of my assignments was to take part in an individual critique with each of three graduate students: one in sculpture, one in painting, one in drawing. All three were women.

I engaged with the work and the artists as I would with any artist. I asked each about her intentions, her challenges, how she would like people to relate to her work, how she saw her work in the world, and so on.

The notable thing about these encounters is that each artist cried. This surprised me, as from my perspective, nothing upsetting had happened. I asked why the women had reacted this way. I learned that each woman had taken part in several prior critique sessions with faculty and visitors, and that each of these had been conflictual and confusing. They had braced for my arrival as if for punishment. Their tears expressed relief.

The first artist described being asked at length to list her influences, and then being told her work was "derivative." This is a silly and common academic double bind, as the framing of conventional education for artists is intrinsically derivative. It is understood that students are influenced by artists who came before them, and their work is seen in the context of art history. As the artists whose studios I visited were therefore encouraged and expected as part of their time at school to offer a lineage of influence, it was troubling that they were then punished for showing it. Perhaps if an artist had grown up in a cave, the resulting work could be immune to being called derivative. The double bind is pervasive, though, because typically art students are also urged to be "original," then left to their own devices to integrate these conflicting expectations.

The second artist was making skillful drawings that expressed her interest in environmentalism, hybrids of humans and animals in imagined settings. Her most recent critique had been with a faculty member, and she was still processing it. He'd accused her of being interested in "mere beauty."

This shocked me. Beauty can be a disguise—"lipstick on a pig." But it can also be a form of healing, a powerful carrier

of meaning. Some art movements have rejected it, preferring a brutal or clumsy aesthetic that avoids beauty's potential seductions. Late in the twentieth century, for instance, there was a long spate of what both makers and critics called "bad painting." But a moment in the art world is simply a moment; you can be sure its opposite will emerge as time goes by. To suggest work that rejects beauty is somehow superior to and more honest or meaningful than the work of an artist who strives for beauty is absurd. To suggest it to an art student who is talented, diligent, and intentional in her work was cruel.

The situation that generates such cruelty is complicated. Art school faculties bring together individuals with remarkably different intentions and reasons for being in their jobs. Regardless of motivation, some—I think most—faculty members care a good deal for their students and invest commensurately. For some others, it's a day job.

Every faculty I've encountered has at least one or two senior members who see themselves as upholding a canon and standards against contemporary onslaughts. In extreme cases, they are perpetually appalled at what colleagues and students are doing, making others as miserable as they can in retribution.

Every faculty has also had members seen as art stars, for whom teaching must coexist with a very full exhibition or performance and residency career. These people tend to be absent more than their colleagues, as they have more opportunities for awards, fellowships, residencies, performances, conferences, and exhibits. When my husband got his MFA in the 1970s, he chose to study at a school that boasted about engaging people he admired as both permanent and visiting faculty. But once on campus, he understood that he would seldom see them, as they were almost always off making or presenting their own work, leaving most classes to teaching assistants—including him. I hear the same complaints today, and the same reasoning—that such artists add luster to the faculty roster and are often inspiring teachers when their schedules allow time, so the trade-offs are worth it.

Every faculty I've encountered has also had members who are passionate about teaching—for many, their chosen primary career—who love their students, and who contribute tremendously to the campus community, offering many additional hours in service to students and to the institution.

Every faculty has had members who see teaching as second-best, having failed to achieve the elite exhibition, publishing, or performance career they desired. Their days are marked by resentment at having to be there at all. These are the faculty members most likely to use critiques as a way to discourage students. Some of them have a sort of "old-boy syndrome," feeling it only right to mete out to their own students the type of tough-love abuse they themselves experienced. This is often justified as preparing students for the difficult working conditions and discouragements they are likely to experience after graduation, "toughening them up" (and thereby grooming them to do the same should they one day be employed to teach). Like sequences of trauma passed through the generations in unhappy families, such repeating patterns help to shape nearly every institution. But I have yet to hear them named as impediments to educational processes. They are just the way things are.

Art Can Be the Practice of Freedom

Art has been my principal path to self-education. What I've learned on a self-directed journey guided by curiosity and desire has often clashed with the ways credentialed experts have understood the same subjects.

Why have I always seen myself as an artist, even before I knew what the word actually meant? Many explanations occur to me; none seems to supersede the others.

There must be a bit of genetic inheritance, as my father had the knack. I can see him in the jumble of our front room: a huge mirror covering one wall to achieve the illusion of space; dusty-pink wallpaper embedded with shiny bits of something resembling sand; a red-and-cream Chinese carved cabinet holding an ancient brass samovar; a little black-and-white TV on a stand. He would move the papers and debris aside to sit at the mahogany dinner table, hunched over a paint-by-numbers canvas. The image was divided into tiny numbered segments, each corresponding to a transparent capsule of paint. He could also sew beautifully, having been apprenticed at thirteen to a tailor in London. I watched him spread turquoise felt over that same dining table, his shears cutting out a circle skirt he then appliquéd with a large furry poodle, de rigueur fashion in the fifties. As a housepainter, he was admired for his ability to create faux finishes, turning ordinary painted woodwork into wood grain or marble.

What really hooked me, though, was the magic: the ability to actualize imagination by drawing it. I didn't much love the world I lived in, but I could draw the one I desired. I knew I had a talent, and I was praised for it. That helped, too.

But where did I acquire the understanding that drew me most powerfully, that art can be the practice of freedom? I think it came from the movies. Growing up, I absorbed Hollywood's idea of the artist—a man, of course. He wore a rakish beret and a navy-and-white-striped French sailor's shirt. He was always strapped for cash, which didn't stop him from spending every evening drinking wine and dancing wildly with a steady stream of bohemian girls. He delighted in thumbing his nose at every convention, and when gripped by inspiration, he painted all night.

By the time I was old enough to live as an artist, the caricature had fallen away, but the pull of freedom endured. Our individual stories might root us in vastly different soil, but we artists form a classless class, welcome in nearly every milieu—a reception at the home of a mogul, a makeshift space on skid row. Wherever we go, most of us can choose to show up as ourselves. But not necessarily to be seen as ourselves. Plenty of privileged people enjoy hobnobbing with artists, boosting their cocktails with tiny shocks to decorum. You have to be willing to accept that as part of the price of a ticket.

Thirty years ago, I was invited to speak at two conferences of the Association of Art Museum Directors, an elite group within an elite universe. The invitations came via the late Marcia Tucker, founder of New York's New Museum, where I'd been a consultant for years. Conferences were typical professional gatherings, talks and workshops punctuated with ceremonial meals and tours of local cultural attractions.

One conference was in Hawaii. Our host's home was entered through a garden, where horses sculpted by Deborah Butterfield grazed; inside, the first thing to see was by installation artist Nam June Paik, a vast number of TV sets playing seven different channels. The other conference was in Dallas–Fort Worth. The mansion's family room was decorated with enormous framed Andy Warhol flowers, six or eight of them side by side. The scale of the furniture had been planned accordingly, so that when I sat for a moment on one of the sectional couches, my feet dangled, making me feel like a misplaced toddler, outside looking in.

My work as a speaker and consultant had gotten me invited to such gatherings, palaces my younger self had never imagined entering. I might show up as myself, but that didn't stop me from being seen as something akin to a fool at court. I was invited—paid—to speak my mind, but what I said about museums' accountability was easily dismissed. These encounters showed me another type of freedom in which money insulates its devotees, not from death or disaster, but from answerability. These were clarifying experiences—two among many—in which the truth of Bob Dylan's "Gotta Serve Somebody" hit home. The excesses of the market, the dulling of art's power by a thick patina of luxury, the belief that art needed to be protected from the people—none of this canceled the freedom I felt.

What does it mean to be educated? One essential answer is to understand our own accountability. These experiences clarified my choice of whom I would serve. My life in art has been fueled by the decision to serve those who seek freedom and too often find the door barred.

The Imperative of Art

Academics tend to have a specialty, a particular period, medium, style. So do many autodidacts. One of the questions that has animated my adult life is this: How do we understand the social value of art? When I first became aware of that question, the clash of relevant perspectives knocked me sideways.

From conservative politicians and pundits, I often heard that art is a frill, a luxury for those who can afford it and like that sort of thing. It matters little compared to what is truly important: taxes, wars, fortunes made or lost. When they think of art, they naturally call to mind the red-carpet institutions embodying the snobbery ridiculed in popular culture. Some of them may be patrons of those institutions, but when it comes to political rhetoric, they tend to condemn them as the province of "limousine liberals."

From the Left, I heard a distinction between base and superstructure, the two main parts of society according to a Marxist analysis. In this framework, base has to do with work and the economy, how labor is divided, conducted, controlled, and the property relations that back it up. Superstructure—roles, rituals, institutions, and so on—emanates from that and is secondary to it. In the circles where I encountered these ideas, a serious person—a serious movement—focused on labor organizing and economic questions, while the rest was left to those less aware, acute, committed.

It's an interesting phenomenon when both the Right and the Left adopt outlooks that deny the centrality of art and culture to the human project and human future.

I realized that I'd have to embark on my own study of the subject. That led me to conclude both perspectives were wrong. What I noticed, what was grounded for me in observation and activism, was art's essential role in our existence. I saw that human communities use song, movement, and other creative ritual to mark both personal and collective moments: births, deaths, marriages, holidays, the anniversaries of important events, and much more. Even in the most extreme circumstances, we act on the desire to make art, scratching images on prison walls; making percussion instruments of our own bodies or whatever comes to hand—iron bars, tin cups; creating a clandestine orchestra in Dachau; smuggling poems and stories past censors at great peril. I saw that books, films, and music can stimulate a robust national debate about questions of justice. I saw people everywhere self-medicating with music as they went about their days, curating playlists to match the challenges they might face. I saw passionate debates about how people are represented in art: Whose statue deserves to stand in the town square? Which actors should play which roles? Who is authorized to tell whose story?

Given such abundant evidence of the necessity of art to human existence, I was struck with particular force by the lengths to which the dominant culture had gone to deny this. Whereas the path of art is nuanced, infinitely mutable, adaptable to even unique personal and social circumstances, ours is a social order based on conformity, mechanization, and quantification. I explored these themes in a pair of 2013 books, the nonfiction *The Culture of Possibility: Art, Artists & The Future,* and a speculative novel approaching the same questions, *The Wave.*

Drawing on science, history, spiritual traditions, educational theories, and other disciplines, in *The Culture of Possibility* I offered twenty-eight arguments for pursuing the public interest in culture. I described the harm our social institutions and both public and private spheres have done in reducing value to what can be counted, weighed, and measured, thereby obscuring cultural value. A long section explored the role of "Corporation Nation" in bringing about this state of affairs, the degree to which the culture of the corporation—emotion, sensation, compassion, beauty, the life of the body all left outside the boardroom—has come to encompass so much of ordinary life. I described a clash of paradigms, calling the two conflicting realities "The Republic of Stories" and "Datastan." Writing those books, my fervent hope was that this conflict would come to light and be resolved. I am still educating myself, still hoping, still cultivating patience.

Students Strike for Knowledge

In my essay on Paul Goodman in Part One, I mentioned the student strike at San Francisco State in 1968, the longest at any university in the United States. I have vivid memories of that time. The on-campus draft-counseling office where I worked remained open at the beginning of the strike. Selective Service wasn't pausing its operations on account of student protest, so for a time, neither did we. For a few weeks, I trod carefully across the campus's wide lawns, past Tactical Squad officers, rifles at the ready, stationed along the edges of flat roofs, past the massive horses that officers rode to corral students intent on breaching the administration building. It was frightening, unreal but real.

Tuition was then free at California's state colleges. Governor Ronald Reagan tried mightily to reverse that, proposing steep cuts to higher education funding. The first change was raising the cost of student fees; before long, tuition was instituted. Earning a degree in that system is still relatively affordable—around seven thousand dollars a year for California residents at the time of this writing. But in the sixties, the cost wasn't much more than the daily fare of an M streetcar ride to the commuter campus in the Sunset District, foggy all summer and much of the rest of the year, too. Waiting for the next young man to come in for counseling, I sat with my feet propped on a tiny space heater to keep warm.

I was a spectator of the strike, not a student. It started with the suspension of George Mason Murray, an English instructor who as minister of education of the Black Panther Party had given speeches that the college trustees found incendiary. Students' ten initial demands included his reinstatement, and also vastly improved access, support, and infrastructure for Black studies. A similar list of ethnic studies demands followed. A new president was appointed, and as his first act, he closed the campus, threatening to invite the police in, a threat he made good. A large group of sympathetic faculty struck in solidarity. After many skirmishes, a settlement was reached that granted enough student demands to end the strike.

What impressed me then as now was the centrality of learning, of the students' passion for knowledge. They struck for classes and programs relevant to their lives and cultural heritages, to protect freedom of expression, to expand the number of faculty of color and the courses they offered. Money wasn't the main issue; the college was affordable, as was obvious from the range of ages, races, ethnicities, and other demographic categories represented on campus each day. When I try to wrap my mind around the intensity of students' desire to bring education in line with lived reality, I feel a deep nostalgia for a time when young people felt their power not only to resist illegitimate authority but to help remake the world.

Learning Is Optional

Our national conversation about education policy treats formal education and learning as if they were one and the same. The default assumption is that anyone who is pulsed through four or more years of higher education will emerge better equipped in key respects: knowing more about the world and how to navigate it, possessing skills and knowledge essential to livelihood. Everyone knows that college endows advantage. But anyone who has taught a college class also knows that it is a matter of individual choice or circumstance whether or not to learn from what is offered.

In the eighties I cotaught a semester-long seminar in a multidisciplinary arts graduate program at San Francisco State University—a decade or so after the student strike described above. The subject was the economic and policy environment for artists' work, and as I've discovered many times since, most of the students, despite years of arts practice and study, were learning about these aspects of the cultural landscape for the very first time.

As part of the preliminary faculty briefing, we were told to be sure to give at least one writing assignment in the course of a semester. There had been a small scandal the prior year when it was discovered that an MFA was awarded to a mature student who was functionally illiterate. Our plan had been to assign reading and writing each week, so we had no problem with this policy (though we did feel taken aback at the need for it, as it suggested a history of indifference to students' actual capabilities).

The students' first assignment was to write a brief paper comparing two essays expressing strongly contrasting views of culture. At the next class meeting, one student—an accomplished young man who had founded an artists' space of some renown—handed in his "paper," which consisted of the two essays cut up and re-arranged into a kind of collage. We handed it back, explaining that the purpose of the assignment was to help him explore, interpret, and respond to both perspec-tives; there was no way to do this without actually passing the words through his own mind and generating his own observations.

The student was furious. He com-plained to the dean. We were given to understand that few of our graduate stu-dents—who had undergraduate degrees from dance, drama, visual arts, and film departments—had been asked to do much reading and writing in the course of their studies. We pressed on.

A Calling or a Career?

When I am invited to speak on a college campus, I like to make myself as available as possible. If the keystone event is a talk for a campus-wide lecture series, I'll also suggest a workshop, offer to visit relevant classes, and say I'll be happy to meet with groups of students or faculty. I like to be busy, I love to talk with people about cul-ture and politics, and I want to offer full value for the fee I am paid.

Those conversations with students are always interesting, allowing me to glimpse their challenges and opportunities. There are always some students agonizing over what they will do after graduation. The agony collects in the spaces between their personal wishes, their feeling of social re-sponsibility, and the questions of livelihood their families keep raising.

This is a particularly vexed question for arts students. Many of them chose their field of study despite parental dis-couragement, "How will you make a living?" being a constant and mostly un-answerable refrain. I've known students who are first-generation in this country, with hardworking immigrant parents who desperately want them to train for careers in health or business, something that promises security and respect. Some earn a degree in one of those professions before they go on to study dance or sculpture, investing tremendous hope and effort in having it both ways. Some find a way to pursue their art but face racking guilt about it. For young people from prosperous back-grounds, the pressure is often less, though the question of livelihood may contribute to the gender disparity in arts degree pro-grams, where females typically greatly out-number males.

Many students in arts majors have had to fight for the legitimacy of their choices. Often, this is a long battle not just with family but with high school coun-selors and the entirety of a commercial culture conditioned to understand profit as a primary human motive. They may be surrounded by people who see work in the same reductive way, effort exchanged for cash. But that's not how these young people see it. Many of them are harboring a secret that animates their persistence and determination: that instead of understanding artmaking as a career, they see it as a calling.

When we meet, I ask about the experiences that ignited their calling. Most everyone has had such experiences: being taken to the theater for the first time and transported to another world; making a mark on paper and entering into a universe of beauty and meaning; raising one's voice or instrument and coming fully into focus. This society does not give art its true value as a transformative practice, a necessary mode of expression, a crucible in which we forge shared values and visions, and a much-needed antidote to social structures that lack heart and soul. These students intuit that understanding of art and are hungry for its expression. It's been whispering in their ears, but they need to hear it spoken aloud, and their curriculum hasn't afforded that opportunity.

I encourage them to recognize their calling as a secret of survival, the state that one of my angels, Abraham Joshua Heschel, called "radical amazement." Artists' capacities—wonder, resourcefulness, social and personal imagination, creativity, resilience, problem solving, a high tolerance for emergence and ambiguity—can be of great value to society, engaging body, emotions, intellect, and spirit. Of course, I also talk with them about questions of livelihood, trying to add to the conventional models—the gallery artist, the repertory actor, the orchestral musician—other ways of working that place their gifts at the service of communities moving toward their own expression and liberation.

Frequently the conversation comes around to this question: "What should I do? What is the most important thing I can do?" I've learned to give one answer, especially to students who are heavily burdened with the challenges of racism, sexism, climate, and poverty and want to make a difference. "You know what you care about and you know what moves you. With that knowledge, do whatever you can that gives you the most pleasure, because that is what will be sustainable."

Unearthing Ethics

What is deemed essential knowledge in a particular field? Formal curricula and syllabi aim to clarify that, though it's a challenging task: Circumstances change, aims change, and ideas of a usable past change, too. My experience with arts students has repeatedly shown me a glaring and serious

omission, one with enormous practical consequences.

I'm not a huge fan of workshops. There's a limit to the value that can be derived from a brief experience, especially if the format is formulaic, as so many are. But there's one workshop I've been glad to present over and over again, at colleges, in organizational settings, at conferences, on Zoom: ethics and values with respect to participatory or community-based arts work.

I am keen to do this because it is needed and missing from every higher education curriculum I have seen. A few hours seem to suffice to motivate many participants to find a path into deeper ethical inquiry as an ongoing practice. The workshop I offer doesn't begin to exhaust the subject, but I have found it can effectively open the subject, which is my aim.

There are many different names for the type of arts work that is the focus here—art for social change, community arts, community cultural development, and more. In this book, I mostly use the term *community-based arts work.* Its common characteristics are collaborative and cocreative process, with process understood to be just as important as product; radical inclusivity and appreciation for differences as key values; ensuring that everyone derives a sense of mastery and ownership from the experience; understanding that the people who make the work and the communities to which they are connected constitute the authenticating audience for it, the best judges of value, beauty, and meaning.

I'm at a loss to understand why every program in higher education preparing people for such work doesn't include at least a full-length course on values and ethics. The need is evident. For practitioners, ethical questions are ever present. As in any enterprise that relies on interaction and collaboration, participants in community-based arts work will see the

world in markedly different ways. An incidental detail for one person can become the foreground and main focus for another. What may be a familiar figure of speech to one person may be a painful insult to another. No one can escape encountering ethical challenges. But they can be ignored and avoided until they explode.

So why don't colleges prepare students to navigate them? And why don't students demand ethics courses? I think there are two main reasons.

The first has to do with the nature of conventional elementary and secondary education. We are trained to want to be perfect, to avoid making mistakes. We don't want to look stupid or become the target of classmates' ridicule. Many people will do anything to avoid being seen as mistaken.

Here's an example: A community-based artist is working with a high school class to paint a mural. Two groups of students prefer different types of music to be playing in the background, each associated with a different cultural milieu—say hip-hop and alt-country. Beyond tussling over who gets to pick, the conflict starts to escalate to name-calling and harassment. For the lead artist trained to be perfect, this is an uh-oh situation, igniting an unpleasant feeling in the pit of the stomach. *Something is wrong! Have I made a mistake? Trouble!* The knee-jerk response is to try to ignore it, chalk it up to indigestion, hope it will go away. Often this wish to avoid mistakes and conflicts persists until a festering issue bursts into full-fledged combat.

In my ethics workshops, I present a framework and a process for understanding and negotiating ethical challenges that arise in the work. Many topics are covered, but the most important message I offer is that ethical challenges will emerge in any group situation. They cannot be avoided entirely. The most powerful and efficacious stance is to accept them as normal and embrace them as occasions for everyone to learn. Instead of "*Uh-oh!*" I always suggest trying for "*Aha! Here's our opportunity!*"

I haven't seen much in higher ed arts curriculum to counteract the avoidance of conflict and cultivate acceptance of ethical challenge. Could the common fear of making mistakes be part of the reason?

The second reason for this inattention to ethics is the likelihood that this void in the curriculum reflects the same gap in faculty members' own experience. The few faculty members I've met who do embrace ethics as a core subject have a depth of community-based experience themselves, so they can speak from lived knowledge. Many can't.

My ethics workshop has two parts. In the first, we talk about the values commonly held by community-based artists and the common ethical challenges they face. I encourage participants to refresh and reconsider their own values, noting that although many of us explore questions of principle when we are young, few regularly revisit bedrock values to see if they have changed with time. I stress that knowing oneself is a prerequisite to working humanely, ethically, and effectively in community. Without self-knowledge, it is impossible to see one's own blind spots and biases, let alone correct for them.

In the second part, participants share ethical challenges in which they were directly involved, and one is picked as a demonstration. These range widely. At one conservative school, students were given individual space to use as they wished in a group show. One student created a floor piece that spelled out obscene words with flowers. (I don't know what the words were, as the student who shared the example was too shy to speak them aloud.) The dilemma presented was whether the floor piece should be censored on the day the mayor came to open the exhibit, for fear it would be so shocking as to jeopardize the school's funding. As the show had already taken place without incident, the example came in handy to illustrate the degree to which preemptive self-censorship precludes actual censorship in the United States, giving participants a chance to ponder their own roles in that phenomenon.

Whatever the example being scrutinized, I lead people to recognize and correct for their own biases or emotional responses before they attempt to understand more deeply. In any conflict between two parties, most people are apt to have an immediate preference. It may be grounded in the partisan way the conflict is presented, in the likability of the parties at odds, or even irrelevant noise—one party reminds me of someone I've clashed with, disposing me to prefer the other.

We look at every situation from as many angles as possible. Often conflicts are presented as merely two-sided, but every conflict has multiple stakeholders: not just the people who painted a wall and the funder who supplied the resources but also those connected to whatever is depicted, the residents of the neighborhood, the parents and teachers of the young people who worked on the painting, and so on. I ask participants to imaginatively assume one of these roles, presenting the relevant perspective such that the person they are standing in for would not feel misrepresented or ridiculed by their account.

This complicates participants' understanding of the issue, enlarging comprehension of who has something at stake and illuminating the dynamic nature of ethics in action. By reducing the polarization that comes with a villain-hero knee-jerk response, it also opens more possibilities for communication, mutuality, and equitable resolution. Some challenges don't yield to

that type of outcome: Sometimes power and privilege throw their weight around at the expense of ordinary people, and wrongs call out to be righted. But even in such a situation, deconstructing multiple dimensions of an issue will increase capacity to navigate it.

Thus far without exception, when I arrive on campus or at a conference or on Zoom to offer some version of the ethics workshop, it is the first time that participants have had this experience.

What does it mean to be educated? Surely it means rehearsing for life, equipping oneself to navigate the challenges common in one's work. But in this field I know best, mostly working with people with abundant formal education, critical ethical skills are largely ignored in curriculum.

Hawking the Highest "Goods"

In oral cultures, proverbs arm their possessors with nuggets of wisdom easily retrieved when earned authority is needed. In citing the wisdom of Solomon, 1 Kings credits him with creating three thousand proverbs. Many autodidacts (including me) collect aphorisms and quotations. Nowadays, they often end up as email signatures. I have two that are almost identical in meaning, the first from the radical Catholic Worker leader Dorothy Day, the second from the Yiddish writer Isaac Bashevis Singer:

> I have long since come to believe that people never mean half of what they say, and that it is best to disregard their talk and judge only their actions.

We know what a person thinks not when he tells us what he thinks, but by his actions.

Both kept coming to mind as I read what a range of academics had to say about their enterprise in the especially beleaguered time of pandemic and its discontents. The following quotation from Agnes Callard, who teaches philosophy at the University of Chicago, appeared in issue 25 of the journal *The Point,* featuring a "symposium" on the university:

> I'll start with what universities are not for. First, they are not for perpetuating the ruling or elite class. Second, they are not for achieving social justice. Doubtless

they do perpetuate the ruling class; many institutions do this. And probably they could do more to bring about social justice. But those things are not what they are for.

Third, universities are not for making money—though they do call for careful financial stewardship. Fourth, they are not for producing better citizens. Fifth, they are not for producing happier human beings.

Callard goes on to say what the university is: "a place where people help each other access the highest intellectual goods."

Following Day's and Singer's advice, I have trouble taking these assertions seriously. They remind me of pharmaceutical companies' distinction between effects (*what we want to sell you*) and side effects (*what happens but we downplay*). No doubt universities are replete with administrators and faculty who have the highest

and purest intentions and do their best to embody and promote them. But if intentions actually mattered more than actions, we wouldn't have the sky-high heaps of collateral damage every social institution produces.

Judged by actions, higher education is all these things, the aspirational as well as the unclaimed. A philosophy department exists alongside a business school named for a polluting corporation; students are trained to heal bodies in one program and to spin public opinion in another. The pursuit of knowledge is not the exclusive province of universities, but they play a huge role in the validation of knowledge—what knowledge counts, how it is legitimately acquired, and by whom. Callard wrote to counter what she saw as scapegoating of the university for society's ills. Fair enough. Among my purposes in writing is to counter the devaluing of lived knowledge pervasive in higher education, and that must be judged not by what is said but by what is done.

The Power of Not Knowing

Most influential historical figures were educated by curiosity. Often their particular genius was to face big questions—even the complex, faceted, confusing challenges dubbed "wicked problems"—with a beginner's mind, without preconceptions, allowing them to discover new perspectives, even solutions. Suzuki Roshi, who founded the first Zen monastery outside Asia and is generally credited with popularizing Zen Buddhism in the United States, said this: "In the beginner's mind there are many possibilities, but in the expert's there are few."

In my experience, awareness of not knowing is more common among the uncredentialed. Consciousness and appreciation of not knowing are valuable aptitudes because they expand possibility. The more certain we are, the more our options narrow. This has been demonstrated. For instance, from 1984 to 2003, the political scientist Philip Tetlock surveyed a large group of political experts—political science professors, journalists, advisers—and students to assess their predictive powers, using clearly measurable questions, such as election outcomes or the outbreak of conflicts. No one can faultlessly foretell the future, no matter how many millions we spend on computer models that purport to do so. But Tetlock found that the least accurate predictions came from those most acknowledged as experts (such as senior professors). They had the most confidence in their own judgment, since it had been praised so often by students and colleagues. As reported in his book *Expert Political Judgment: How Good Is It? How Can We Know?* the best predictors were students themselves, many of whom had the humility to know what they didn't know.

Prior to the twentieth century, small numbers of mostly men attended universities. The more common path to accomplishment was to follow an elementary education by learning a trade and engaging in some form of apprenticeship, whether self-guided or under another's tutelage. Even at today's most prestigious institutions of higher learning, curricula are peppered with works by people who did not possess degrees but whose accomplishments continue to make them essential sources of knowledge.

The assumed superiority of formal education—not only for those who pursue necessary technical training in professions such as science, law, or engineering but also for those whose materials are ideas, words, images, and feelings—seems remarkably arbitrary unless we understand it as a sorting mechanism for a class system. Surely everyone's offerings deserve to be judged on actual skill, knowledge, and impact, and not on what the person did to acquire those things. Credentialism as we experience it in the United States today reveals the extent to which, when it comes to education, elitism has outpaced respect for wisdom.

Exiting the Anthology

Academia as an enterprise is shot through with customs and practices that assert its monopoly on knowledge, such as the peculiar nature of academic publishing. Here's one story.

A few years ago, I stopped accepting invitations to contribute to academic anthologies. These were books edited by professors I knew and included chapters by a range of academics and practitioners in fields I was connected to: case studies of community-based arts work, essays on cultural policy, and so on. I had three main reasons for stopping.

My first reason had to do with the inequity of these projects. Although the contributing faculty members were supported by their salaries and the resulting publishing credits helped them achieve tenure or honors, I, like other nonacademic contributors, was not compensated in any way. The editors certainly didn't become rich from these publications, but they did receive royalties, however small. The editors I worked with felt themselves to be liberalizing curriculum by inviting nonacademics to contribute, and on the face of it, this is a good thing, validating different paths to knowledge. But none of them acknowledged that nonacademic contributors would be subsidizing their own participation. I knew this when I accepted such invitations but went ahead anyway, thinking the books would provide avenues for wider exposure of my ideas and that would be worth my time.

My second reason was an academic convention I found both silly and unethical. The last chapter I wrote before deciding to stop was about the evaluation of community-based work, specifically the inadequacy of quantifiable data to convey the real value of work that was relational, fluid, emergent, and long-term. The chapter was based on decades of direct experience. The editors asked for only one major change before publication. They wanted me to cite other authors' names as sources for my ideas and observations, using a common academic style. I was asked to go back through my manuscript and add a list of authors and titles at the end, then insert parenthetical last names from the list at points in the text where their ideas were relevant.

It's not that no one else had written about the things that interested me. To the contrary, I had footnoted sources when I quoted or referred directly to one. But as the chapter in question was based on personal experience and observation, it simply wasn't accurate to credit others with the ideas I discussed.

This custom goes straight to the heart of the questions I raise in this book. In academic convention, ideas are validated when they are authorized by other scholars. Yes, there is nothing new under the sun; something close to whatever you or I may think has almost certainly been thought before. But not every correlation is causative, and what's more, coincidence happens. Just as Charles Darwin and Alfred Russel Wal-

lace independently posited the theory of evolution, you or I might have something to say about, for instance, evaluation—something that was derived from our own observation rather than the work of others but was aligned with that work. If we'd never come across the book or paper in question, if we were unfamiliar with the author, would it be right to list that person in the text? I didn't think so. I thought asking me to do that was a way of framing my contribution as imitative rather than presenting it on its own merits. I thought it was a way to convert lived knowledge to credentialed expertise, thus sanitizing it for academic use.

My third reason was recognizing that my own rationale for contributing to these anthologies had been ungrounded. Each book was released by an academic publisher with a cover price unaffordable for most individual buyers. I am told that these are the economics of academic publishing—small print runs, limited readership; think of it as stocking college libraries—and unavoidable, as it is necessary to go with one of the recognized academic publishers because that will redound to the contributing academics' credit and facilitate ordering by universities.

Right now, I'm looking at Palgrave Macmillan's page for one of the anthologies to which I contributed. I can buy a print version of the book for 125 euros (approximately $150 at the time of this writing); readers can download my thirteen-page chapter for a paltry 25 euros ($30 at the time of this writing). I doubt the book has found much of an audience beyond the authors' own classes and the few reviewers who blurbed it. It certainly has had no noticeable impact on the dissemination of my ideas. Considering this, when I tried to parse the logic of writing without compensation but with unearned attribution for people who can afford $150 texts, I had to admit defeat.

Trickle-Down Distortion

Some institutions are intrinsically damaging or corrupt. The fossil fuel industry's lobbying group spends millions of dollars each year persuading elected officials to ignore climate crisis, placing oil companies' short-term financial interests above concern for life on the planet. Others are rooted in positive intentions but can be pushed off course by countervailing forces. Higher education is in this category. In the chapter that follows, I chose to write about the ambitions, biases, and compromises that have distorted this field because they have a ripple effect: When a much-respected and honored university's practices magnify the worship of wealth and entrenched power and the disparagement of lived knowledge, the resulting deformation doesn't stop at the campus boundaries. It influences and infiltrates public opinion, and that shapes action in the world. The glow of virtuous worthiness clinging to higher education in the popular imagination helps to deflect awareness of its shortcomings. This is sad, because those shortcomings can easily be corrected, but not unless they are acknowledged. As my angel James Baldwin said, "Not everything that is faced can be changed, but nothing can be changed until it is faced."

I wrote in Part One about my high school counselor, a kind and wise man who was generous with his time and tissues. I got into quite a bit of trouble in high school for refusing to conform to the rules. Two transgressions led to repeated visits to the counselor's office. First, I refused to recite the Pledge of Allegiance each morning, hand on my heart, facing the flag that hung in each classroom. The Pledge was formally adopted by Congress in 1945; the words *under God* were inserted into it in 1954, at the height of the Red Scare, when I was in second grade. I recited it for years. But by the time I entered high school, the whole exercise reminded me of the anti-Soviet and anti-Chinese propaganda films we were shown, in which rows of compliant students repeated some form of loyalty oath. It offended my idea of freedom.

Second, I refused to take part in "duck-and-cover" air-raid drills—we called them "bomb drills"—which were a regular part of school life, just like fire drills. In the 1951 federal civil defense film we students were shown, Bert the Turtle was a role model, telling us what to do "when the flash comes." I learned elsewhere that within a blast radius of about three kilometers, virtually everything would be incinerated. That convinced me that the primary function of the exercise was to normalize the atomic bomb, ensuring that we would die quietly beneath our desks.

I remember sitting in my counselor's office, complaining bitterly about how—despite endless lectures on liberty and justice—everyone refused to admit how repugnant these rituals were, let alone acknowledge how they inculcated compliance to authority that might not be legitimate. I must have said it like this, all florid righteousness and injured innocence: "Haven't they heard of McCarthy? Haven't they heard of Hiroshima? What a bunch of hypocrites!" He handed me the Kleenex box, smiling. "You just want people to be reasonable," he said. "You just want them to do what they say." I nodded, feeling understood. Those seemed to be fair desires. "I wonder when you will stop expecting that," he continued.

I never have. I have heard that certain personality traits can be changed with time and diligence, but not all of them, and for me, not this one. When I look back at my story, I see that one persistent theme has been the refusal to play the game, conform to the rules, kiss up to the enforcers. I'd like to take this as a badge of honor, but truly, it just *is,* not a choice, but something I've come to accept as the way I am. It hasn't stopped me from feeling sorry for myself when the hands I bite decline to feed me. I've sometimes envied people I know who are so good at currying favor, sanding the sharp edges off their criticisms or silencing them altogether, making everyone—including me—feel like the most interesting person in the room. That's their superpower, and this is my not so super counterpart.

So yes, formal education accomplishes many good and important things, and provides many people with positive and useful experiences. But I just want educational institutions, their advocates, and anyone else who has ever espoused equity, empathy, or justice to do what they say. I'm hoping that you, unlike my beloved counselor, won't find that an impossible dream.

14

Education Challenged

Money Changes Everything

As I wrote this book, I saw ever-greater connections between each challenge I observed and the structure and informing values of the U.S. economy. On the most basic level, if as a society we prize the lives and contributions of the wealthiest—so that a cosmetic surgeon or a corporate CEO is understood to have *earned* multimillions, while it is deemed fitting that a teacher or medical aide scrapes by—our sense of value has been distorted by the worship of wealth. If we persist in being so strongly biased in favor of credentialed expertise and the quantifiable (no matter how much it leaves out), we cheat ourselves of the creative thinking of the noncredentialed. If we remain imprisoned by the protective fence formal education has placed around approved knowledge, I doubt we will be able to learn our way out of our collective mess.

Parables help me understand. Yiddish literature is replete with tales of the town of Chelm in which the denizens, seen by their neighbors as wise, were actually prize fools, repeatedly attempting to solve problems in ways that made them worse. A classic tale has the people of Chelm building a new synagogue, first digging the foundation. Someone asks what they will do with the huge pile of dirt thus created. One of their sages suggests digging another pit to bury it. Someone points out that they will then have to dispose of the dirt created by the second dig. Finally they hit on a solution: make the second pit twice as large as the first, to hold everything!

What the Chelmniks can never see is the big picture, how the impact of each action doesn't stop with whatever happens next; how a chain of prior unthought-out decisions created their plight; how tracing each action into the future can influence what is done today; how tracing a decision tree back to its roots may actually yield helpful alternatives.

As it is with Chelm, so it is with the United States.

Our national default setting offers a cost-benefit analysis as the primary tool for every job. What can't be quantified isn't

117

deemed worthy of consideration. If the goal is to create the maximum number of housing units for the least money, for example, people wind up being warehoused in cramped, shoddy quarters. But if the lead criteria for housing policy are humane values—comfort, safety, harmony, beauty, and conviviality—very different solutions emerge.

I often think of the great sociologist and progressive activist C. Wright Mills, who wrote of the American proclivity to treat public issues as private troubles. When someone loses a job, instead of looking at structural changes in the field or policies that shape overall employment prospects, a typical response is to wonder what that person did to deserve being let go. This personalization of social issues is epidemic, and it speaks directly to the question of what it means to be educated. How many people would rather ignore the skyrocketing costs of higher education and the profits of private colleges coexisting with repeated cuts to funding for public education and focus instead on the profligacy of students facing debt, suggesting credit counseling and better budgeting as the remedy? As a nation, we look the other way at stupendous medical debt, though the average cost of care for U.S. residents is double that of comparable countries, while health outcomes are far poorer. Our systems are broken. Yet our mainstream discourse tends to see this state of affairs as given and unchangeable, a bumper crop of private troubles.

Like the townspeople of Chelm, we repeat the same inadequate responses to our challenges, as if they hadn't already failed. We go on digging bigger and bigger pits without ever looking at why we started and what we are going to do with the dirt. Many of those empowered to offer possible solutions to massive problems constrain their thinking to approaches that don't disrupt the status quo distribution of economic and social power. This rotten consensus makes them fear risking a new approach, one that may disrupt cherished assumptions or offend the powerful. But they seem quite content to go on failing in the same old ways, those already vetted and approved for their role in perpetuating the profit-first status quo, treating people without economic privilege as unavoidable collateral damage.

Why has higher education become so problematic? My understanding is pretty straightforward, though its manifestations are many and complex. We are living in a society that has allowed social goods to become primary profit centers, and the resulting polarization of wealth and privilege is killing us. The valorization of financial success has a dark side in the widespread tendency to punish people for their poverty. I'm not talking only about the rituals of humiliation and debasement forced on applicants for social assistance or about the gang of landlords who waited for the pandemic eviction moratorium to end so tenants could be displaced in favor of prosperous gentrifiers. We also see this in everyday interactions, when the next person in line at the grocery store berates a mother for buying her children ice cream with food stamps. Education is just one place where profit taking has come to

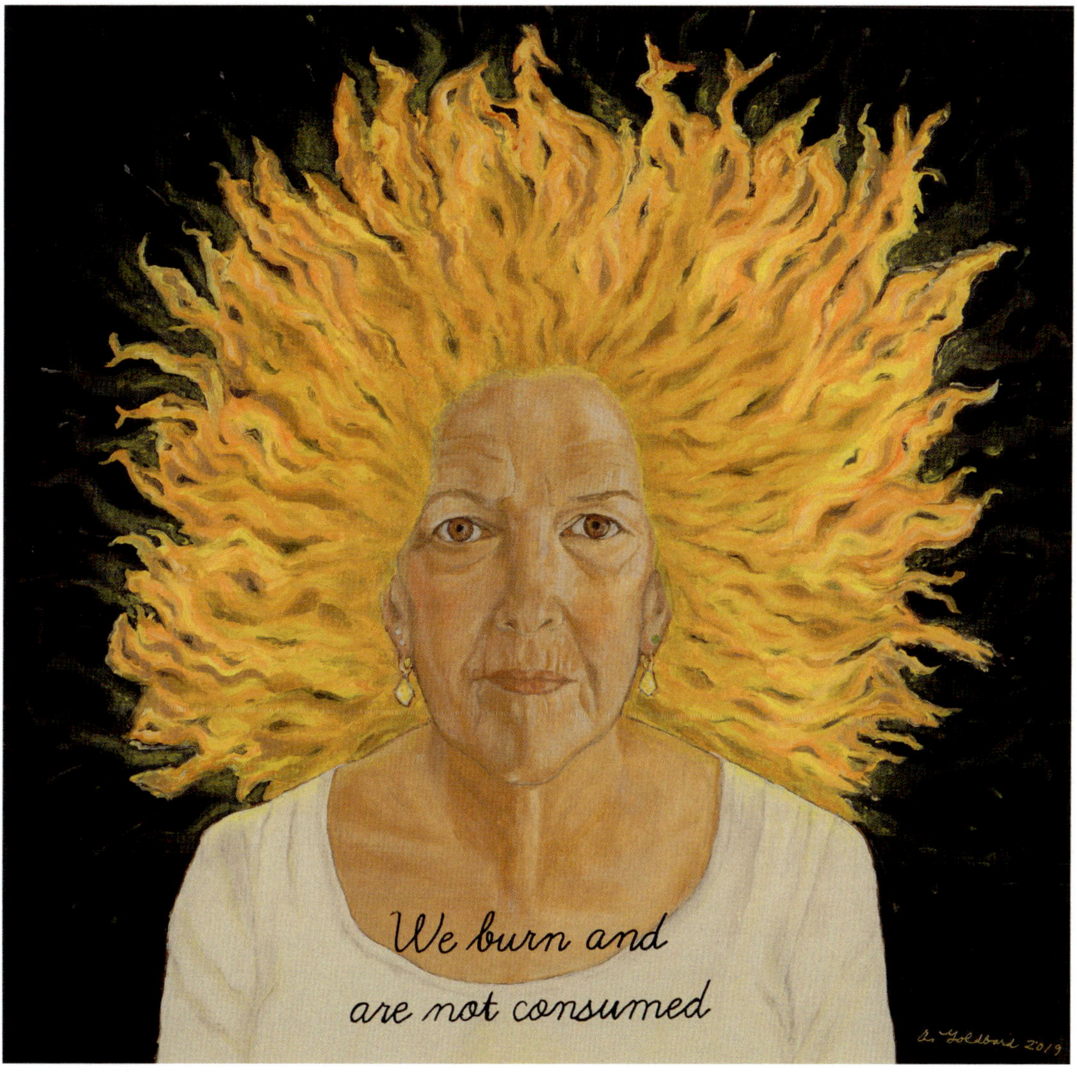

"We Burn," 24 x 24 inch oil on panel from the 2019 series, "Gaia and Shekhina Speak."

trump social well-being, but it is an illuminating focal point because the contradictions are massive. Along with housing and health, education has become a bleeding edge of social collapse. Seeing it clearly can be a step toward showing us the way out.

What Everyone Knows

In this chapter, I explore ways of thinking about education that have colonized public opinion, downplaying the questions that ought to be asked in favor of accepting a default reality—*what everyone knows.*

I want readers to consider what it means to be educated without jumping to ready-made answers that don't serve the inquiry.

Before I explore some of the developments that convince me we need to rethink what it means to be educated, I want to describe the feelings behind my desire to share them. Most important to me is directing attention to the loss of human skill, knowledge, and creativity that results when people succumb to the fiction that only credentialed knowledge is worthy of respect.

Have you ever shared a restaurant meal with a person—someone in possession of blue-ribbon credentials who accepts the deference they confer as due and seemly— who is so rude to the wait staff that you must speak up, or at least make some ameliorating gesture, extra thanks, smiles, a big tip? Or if your companion is someone you feel you can't correct, you merely cringe and try to make your excuses early?

What if people behave appropriately but harbor notions that diminish others? The people who fix your plumbing or serve you lunch—do you see them as dismissible except for the convenience of their necessary duties? Can you imagine them as engaged with the life of the mind—devising a new and useful invention, writing a play about the gig economy, scheming how to bring an exciting new restaurant to life, reading the latest information on climate science? Some of them may have advanced credentials, while others may have learned on the job; either way, their job status may make them vulnerable to disrespectful treatment. I think of Representative Alexandria Ocasio-Cortez (having earned a cum laude degree in international relations and economics), who was employed as a bartender before she ran for office. How many customers insulted her intelligence before she emerged as a brilliant public phenomenon?

I have worked as a clerk in a clothing shop and behind a coffee bar. These experiences were humbling in an instructive way: I was young and outspoken; having to stick to polite banter allowed me to see how inconsequential I could seem to others and therefore to myself. But there were also opportunities to subvert the situation. I played at sizing up a customer, then saying the right things to flatter her into buying the clothes she was trying on. I told myself I never did it unless it was true, but remembering now, I can see it felt like getting my own back if someone had been dismissive or rude. There was once a show of my paintings on the walls of the coffee bar where I brought people drinks and snacks. For the run of the exhibit, during my shift I eavesdropped on patrons' conversations about the portraits, sometimes choosing a moment to say that I had painted them. I was interested in the flavors of astonishment my revelation produced.

How would our experience be different if everyone was given the same benefit of the doubt regardless of wealth, power, or credentials? What if, heedless of your own social or educational status, you approached every encounter as holding the same potential for revelation, connection, liberation? What if everyone you met approached you in this way?

Our addiction to credentialism has many impacts. Worst of all is the fact that in a class system that worships thieves and liars, too many write off half the world for lacking the desire or means to ante into the merit-for-money game. This injures those written off, to be sure. It also deprives everyone else of the wisdom they might contribute to our collective predicament. The system depends on squandering the potential of vast numbers so as to enhance the fortunes of the few. This makes me angry and breaks my heart. What does it do to you?

The Education Myth

Everyone knows that education is the panacea for all social ills. A typical conversation among my friends goes this way:

Friend #1: "I can't believe so many people voted for Trump. I blame it on the schools. Don't they teach kids to think anymore?"

Friend #2: "Most of the MAGA people didn't go to college. And that's who's determining the fate of this country!"

These people believe higher education equals liberal values. But Ph.D.s are as thick on the ground on the Right as on the Left. If you see yourself as progressive and believe that being educated means sharing your own values, think again. In the 2016 presidential election, 49 percent of college graduates voted for Clinton, 45 percent for Trump. In the 2020 election, the gap was wider, with about 56 percent of college graduates voting for Biden (or, as many commentators have pointed out, against Trump). But neither gap is wide enough or understood enough to justify concluding that education equals progressive values.

There's a circular logic to this argument. Analysts frequently blame what's called the "education gap" for the migration of a significant number of working-class voters to Trump. In September 2021, Ruy Teixeira, a Democratic pundit, wrote an oft-quoted piece entitled "There Just Aren't Enough College-Educated Voters!" I agree with his point that Democrats' binary is

wrong: Neither assuming that the loyalty of working-class voters of color is permanent nor writing off white working-class Trump voters as a lost cause seems to be working. But the "education gap" mistakes correlation for cause. Just because voting patterns map to educational attainment doesn't mean voters are sorting themselves that way. Formal education often maps to occupation. Trump's pledge to bring back working-class jobs, however hollow I may find it, surely influenced voters who imagined themselves benefiting from his election.

This much is indisputable: That furious person in the red hat storming the Capitol on January 6, 2021, may well have had a pocketful of degrees.

Many of the political thinkers who shaped the U.S. Right's philosophies went to elite colleges. Before being recruited by the CIA and writing a book-length defense of Senator Joseph McCarthy, William F. Buckley, Jr., collected many honors at Yale. The consultants who masterminded Trump's campaign, the policy wonks who feed ideas and frameworks to elected officials on the far right, are all credentialed by higher education, many at prestigious schools. Steve Bannon (Trump's erstwhile chief strategist) graduated from Virginia Tech, then received a master's degree from Georgetown University and a second master's from Harvard Business School. Many extreme-right politicians are similarly credentialed: Texas senator Ted Cruz graduated from Princeton and went on to Harvard Law, where he earned his J.D. magna cum laude. Senator Tom Cotton graduated from Harvard, where he also obtained his law degree. Mike Pompeo (who served as both CIA director and secretary of state under Trump) went to West Point, then received his J.D. at Harvard.

It would be easy to put together long lists of liberal politicians and consultants with similar educational credentials. I'm not suggesting that colleges breed only certain political views or loyalties. My point is that formal education is not a reliable remedy for xenophobia, racism, or a proclivity to make one's associates rich at public expense.

When my friends tout education as the cure for whatever fresh political hell is under discussion, what are they really saying? Some, at least, are expressing the belief that when people disagree with them, the problem must be a lack of information or comprehension. I love to discuss ideas, including political ideas, but my least favorite conversation is with someone who shares that perspective and therefore repeats a thesis until I want to run screaming. If I don't run, there comes a point where I have to say, "You know, I really do understand what you're saying, but I see it differently. Would you like me to mirror back what I heard so you can check me?" Sometimes the response is astonishment; the speaker simply can't compute how I might actually have heard and understood yet failed to have been persuaded.

Is this an expression of personality, a by-product of an approach to education in which received knowledge is understood to be self-evident, a disinclination to question one's assumptions, or some type of cognitive inability to consider differing views? I only know that everyone is free to read the same books or listen to the same lectures and come away with opposite views. Values provide the foundational factor, shaping what the French philosopher Lucien Goldmann called "potential consciousness." What you and I already believe makes it difficult for us to let in contradictory information. And as individuals—whether we dropped out, squeaked through school, or graduated with honors—we believe very different things.

Redemption Romance

The dominant view of higher education as the superior—sometimes only—route to knowledge and wisdom is shaped by beliefs in intrinsic virtues for which very little evidence can be cited. For example, that academia is a meritocracy, that talent will be recognized and rewarded regardless of who possesses it. In the spirit of these times, the best-loved stories speak of redemption, but with a flavor that reinforces the myth of meritocracy. The homeless kid who graduates from Harvard with honors, the abandoned child of addicts who becomes a surgeon, the former inmate who now coaches millionaires—the person who hits bottom or begins there, and by dint of tremendous sacrifice and ambition is elevated and embraced, achieving the rich rewards of the American dream, all of it due to the institution that opened its arms.

These stories come around each year when college acceptances are doled out. In 2019, Akintunde Ahmad wrote in *The Atlantic* about the capricious fortunes that got his brother imprisoned and him into Yale, an accomplishment celebrated with an appearance on *The Ellen DeGeneres Show.* "My story is told as though it is a positive one, inspirational," he wrote. "But I see it as a grim one, the tale of a harsh reality that wrecks people. There is nothing positive about classifying me as an exception. When a person is exceptional for doing what I have done, the whole system is cruel to its core."[1]

The idealized view of higher education has become more and more ludicrous as the real social and economic relations behind deciding whose path to a Ph.D. will be paved most smoothly have been exposed. In this chapter, I point out some of the harms this has engendered, not just for autodidacts but for nearly everyone.

College for All

Free higher education is an excellent social program. I admire the policies of countries such as Finland, Germany, Iceland, and Norway that have implemented tuition-free public college. They see formal education as a social good, not a profit center. If legislation similar to that first introduced in 2017 by Senator Bernie Sanders and Representative Pramila Jayapal had been passed, it would have made four-year public college tuition-free for families earning less than $125,000 a year and for students at historically Black colleges and other named categories, made community college and two-year tribal colleges free for all, and expanded Pell Grants to students, major steps in the same direction. The bill has been repeatedly reintroduced; S.1288 was referred to committee in 2021 and as of this writing remains there.

Sanders and Jayapal are obviously not seeing this legislation as the leading edge of social justice but, rather, as a necessary component. But throughout recent election campaigns, instead of a broad class-conscious program that really would change conditions for vast numbers, some candidates and advocates have touted "college for all" as an economic and social panacea. Before I explore whether college for all is up to that task, let's inquire into the idea's possible future.

What stands in the way of such legislation being adopted? For one thing, the profit-driven character of U.S. private (and some public) colleges makes clear that education here is equated with economic power, and that is a power that elite institutions don't want to diminish. Although many students receive some type of financial aid to lower their actual costs, the average annual tuition and fees for private colleges in 2020–2021 was $35,000 (up to $52,000 for Harvard, and nearly $58,000 for Yale). For out-of-state enrollees at public colleges, it was just over $21,000; and for in-state attendees of public schools, $9,700.[2]

For specialized programs, costs can be much higher. At the Wharton School of the University of Pennsylvania, first-year tuition and fees for the MBA program amounted in 2021–2022 to $83,230. Does embedding oneself in one of the richest higher-education institutions skew perceptions of value? Early in 2022, Assistant Professor Nina Strohminger asked her Wharton students how much the average American makes a year in wages.[3] The resulting tweet and story went viral because a quarter of her students guessed six figures, one guessing as high as $800,000.

The most prestigious institutions have heaped up remarkably large endowments: more than $38 billion for Harvard, $29 billion for Yale, $26 billion apiece for Stanford and Princeton, for example. It would be absurd to think people equate these riches with the fortunes of their local community college or land-grant school. But it's not a mistake to see blue-ribbon colleges as enclaves of wealth.

As a way to accomplish its stated goal of widening access to higher education by reducing economic obstacles, college for all makes perfect sense. But as a political program to address inequality, it fails to pass the commonsense test. I have yet to hear politicians draw a straight and convincing line between college for all and a decent, humane society guaranteeing basic social goods to everyone. How could they?

The Skewed Math of Educational Value

For people who work in factories, service jobs, in construction—in wage-based fields where the 70 percent of those without a four-year college degree are supervised by degree holders unlikely to have themselves performed the tasks their credentials supposedly qualify them to oversee—being told that college for all is the solution equals being told you are insufficient, your work is unworthy, and, sadly, it is probably too late for you to do anything about it.

The people who are leaning into the college-as-panacea message are all college graduates, to be sure. Whether or not they consciously intend it, one clear message that comes across is aspirational, with themselves as the objects of admiration and imitation: *I'm successful. I went to college. Be like me!*

The other obvious message is a sad reproach to their claims for the efficacy of education: They don't seem to be able to do simple math. Put plainly, the economic value of a college education depends on its scarcity. People who point out that a college education increases earning power don't seem to notice that it does so by valuing the work of college graduates over the work of everyone else. If college for all suddenly became a universal policy—significantly increasing the number of people who receive bachelor's degrees in any given year—the pressure to obtain master's degrees would grow. The bar would have to be raised to preserve the scarcity that confers economic advantage. In fact, this is already well under way. A decade ago, Debra W. Stewart, then president of the Council of Graduate Schools, told *The New York Times,* "Several years ago it became very clear to us that master's education was moving very rapidly to become the entry degree in many professions."[4]

Everyone agrees that higher education–based economic advantage is real, but it is hard to quantify with precision. The statistics show a significant increase in compensation with a bachelor's degree compared to a high school diploma, judged by either mean or average income. But means and averages don't reveal all that much. Graduates who get jobs at stock brokerages, energy companies, engineering firms, or advertising agencies drive the average up even as the pool contains all those college graduates who work as retail clerks, in hotels and restaurants, or as teachers or social workers. Graduates who live in high-paying regions such as San Francisco, Silicon Valley, New York, or Seattle drive the average up even as the pool also contains all those who live in Arkansas, Alabama, West Virginia, or Mississippi, among the lowest-paying states. Individuals in these categories may hold the same job with the same qualifications but receive very different salaries, with different buying power.

I applaud the quest for knowledge, whether undertaken in elite institutions, community colleges, public libraries, or the privacy of one's own home. But touting college for all as a cure for inequality positions higher education primarily as the quest for income. This cultural meaning—the taint of elitism clinging ever more strongly to higher education—is a major obstacle to a democratic future.

Reality Check

Look at the reality of higher education versus the college-for-all ideal. While 70 percent of high school graduates enter college, a large number of first-generation college students drop out, many after the first year, others along the way.[5] This is arguably because their appallingly underfunded and inadequately imagined K–12 educations have not prepared them to succeed in that system, particularly if they face racism and class prejudice. Instead of focusing on correcting this widespread deficiency, college for all has become the focus. Meanwhile, U.S. school districts typically and consistently spend significantly less educating poor children than children from wealthier communities. Students' economic disadvantage carries through higher education and beyond, where those from low-income families definitely earn more than their peers possessing only high school diplomas, but far less than their fellow college graduates from wealthier families.

The college-for-all argument focuses much more on leveling the field for entry than on the massive improvements in K–12 education that would prepare students to stay in college or the rethinking of college education and campus life that would support them in a sustained and satisfying formal educational experience. It also ignores removing obstacles to recognizing the value of lived experience and self-education.

Most important (though virtually absent from mundane political discourse) is rethinking work and compensation. This could bring income in line with social value and vastly reduce the scope and impact of rent-seeking—amassing excess wealth without creating new opportunity, as by lobbying for new regulations that will give you a greater share of the market than your competitors. Health insurance is a good example: Drug and insurance companies lobby for the end of the Affordable Care Act to increase their profitable market share. The income tax system is a better example: The wealthy have lobbied successfully for a system of taxation that results in billionaire investor Warren Buffett, as he's often quoted as saying, being taxed at a lower rate than his secretary.

Wealth concentration at the end of 2021 was higher than at any time since World War II.[6] The immoral, egregious wealth inequality that has the richest 1 percent owning 38 percent of U.S. wealth while the poorest 40 percent own a fraction of 1 percent was created in large part by reshuffling the economic deck to deal the best hands to the haves, greatly expanding their wealth without having to create a single job. Meanwhile, approximately half of those deemed essential workers make less than the fifteen dollars per hour Congress has thus far refused to ratify as the minimum wage. Why doesn't rethinking work and compensation and supporting working-class well-being earn more attention than college for all?

That disparity may help answer a question many progressives find baffling: Why have so many working-class people voted against their own apparent economic interests, supporting Trump, for instance, a plutocrat whose presidential agenda was to enrich the members of his own class at ordinary people's expense? To ask this question is to imply that the Democratic Party is the party of working people, of economic democracy, and should by rights have captured their votes. To be fair, if the Republican Party is the benchmark, they have a solid point. But is that a reasonable standard? Many voters don't see Democrats accomplishing all that much to loosen the grip of privilege on the ship of state. I imagine many of them fail to see a connection between college for all and their own future well-being. Instead, they may see privileged people positioning themselves as aspirational role models. As a political platform, not so appealing.

Scamming the System

Everyone knows that possession of a formal education confers a head start on the road to economic and social success. This truth has come to seem so self-evident that parents go to remarkable lengths to procure the highest of higher education for their children, to advance them to the head of the line.

In March 2019, headlines proclaimed that federal prosecutors had charged fifty individuals in six states with participating in a large-scale, high-end scheme to help students gain admission to prestige schools—Yale, Stanford, and the University of Southern California were mentioned most often—to ensure students a blue-chip diploma despite lackluster qualifications. The Justice Department said this was the largest college admissions prosecution in history, involving two hundred federal agents.

Most of those indicted were parents of high school students. Some were celebrities. All were wealthy and unscrupulous enough to spend up to a million dollars and beyond to circumvent official admission policies. William Singer, founder of the college preparatory network at the center of the scandal, received $25 million in bribes between 2011 and 2019, much of it to help students masquerade as top athletes, but also to manipulate test results, alter racial classifications, or claim disability exemption, thus enabling these students to receive preferential treatment. Some accounts say that students were unaware of their parents' actions. For example, some students took their own SAT tests, leaving the completed tests with proctors who had been bribed to change their answers to achieve the desired scores. Were they pleasantly surprised when the scores arrived, content to assume they'd underestimated their own abilities? In other cases, impostors were hired to take the tests on students' behalf; how could that have happened without students' knowledge?

Two celebrities charged in this scandal were released, to considerable publicity, after serving short prison terms. The actress Felicity Huffman, a small fry in this story, spent fifteen thousand dollars to raise her daughter's SAT scores. She was released in October 2019, eleven days into her fourteen-day sentence. Actress Lori Loughlin and her fashion designer husband, Mossimo Giannulli, paid Singer half a million dollars to gain admission for their two daughters to USC by having the girls impersonate athletes. The couple denied the charges for a year, but they eventually pled guilty in exchange for two-

and five-month prison sentences, respectively. Both performers were at first dropped by television and film outlets, but shortly after her release, Huffman was cast in a new sitcom pilot, and in September 2021, Loughlin was cast in a Hallmark Christmas special. All of the thirty-three indicted parents either pled guilty or were convicted. Custodial sentences ranged from a few weeks to a few months. Many sentences included required hours of community service. Fines ranged from $9,500 to $250,000.

How to evaluate these consequences? In the U.S. criminal justice system many people are serving long sentences—in some cases, life—for petty thefts, drug possession, and similar offenses. Less than a decade ago, the ACLU published a report detailing more than three thousand cases of individuals serving life without parole, most for small nonviolent drug offenses. Do the penalties meted out in this college admissions scandal seem, in contrast, remarkably kind to the privileged people who committed these crimes? Without a doubt.

In December 2020, Loughlin's daughter Olivia Jade, a highly successful social media "influencer" (if not an actual honor student), said this on "Red Table Talk," a Facebook talk show hosted by Jada Pinkett-Smith: "I remember thinking, 'How are people mad about this?'" she said. "Like, I know that sounds so silly, but in the bubble that I grew up in, I didn't know so much outside of it, and a lot of kids in that bubble, their parents were donating to schools and doing stuff that advantaged—so many advantages. It's not fair and it's not right, but it was happening."

How to Cut in Line

It might be nice to think of the 2019 scandal as an aberration, but it would also be false. At the time of these arrests, the cost of yearly tuition and fees at Yale was nearly $55,000—and Yale isn't the most expensive school. As many as 30 percent of admissions at the types of institutions targeted are "legacies," the children (or nieces, nephews, grandchildren) of graduates who are given preference in admissions, such as overlooking poor grades or test scores, or leaning heavily on factors perceived to be compensating, such as letters of recommendation testifying to sterling personal characteristics.

When that way to cut in line isn't available, a large donation can get the job done. Jared Kushner's father pledged $2.5 million to Harvard at the time his underachieving son applied for admission, and despite grades and test scores far below that institution's general standards, he was admitted. Absent these means of influencing college admissions, parents with money can pay for private tutors, send their children to high-priced college-prep coaching programs, pile on private lessons to help their children excel in elite sports such as rowing or water polo, or secure the services of a professional college-admissions essay ghostwriter.

A 2019 study of Harvard admissions found that more than 43 percent of white students admitted were "recruited athletes, legacies, those on the dean's interest list [i.e., "applicants . . . of special importance to the dean of admissions"] and children of faculty and staff (ALDCs)," in contrast to fewer than 16 percent of students of color. The researchers indicated that of the white ALDCs, "roughly three-quarters would have been rejected" if the criteria as applied to students of color had been used to consider their applications.[7]

Seen from this perspective, to be educated is to receive a gilt-edged ticket to ride. Formal education channels young people into categories of status and privilege according to their means. While the 2019 indictments provoked outrage, legacy preferences and indirect forms of bribery, such as the gift that eased Jared Kushner's path to Harvard, mostly do not. They appear ordinary.

Everyone knows this is just the way things are. In fact, paving the way for the privileged seems so normal and usual that many of the same people who look the other way when wealthy parents ensure their children's entry to elite schools are outraged at the existence of preferences—such as those based on race—that make some small room for non-elites at those same institutions. Their outrage plugs into a skewed frame of fairness. In this alternate reality, beneficiaries of affirmative action are getting away with something, while everyone else must follow the rules and work hard, yet still may be bumped out of line by an undeserving Black or Latino student. The outrage persists despite abundant evidence that the system is intrinsically unfair, the opposite of an unrigged contest of effort and talent, one in which undeserving advantage repeatedly beats hard work.

As I write, a large group of plaintiffs awaits the Supreme Court's ruling on whether to hear an appeal of their lawsuit charging Harvard with discriminating against Asian American applicants. Asian Americans (a broad and diverse group) make up less than 6 percent of the U.S. population, and more than 25 percent of current admissions to Harvard. The suit alleges that based on grades and test scores, to be truly fair, that percentage should be much higher. In 2019, a federal district court judge ruled that Harvard does not discriminate, and the ruling was upheld by the U.S. Court of Appeals. Many civil rights organizations have taken Harvard's side, arguing that the already disproportionate representation of Asian Americans satisfies fairness, and that expanding it would effectively overturn affirmative action for historically marginalized groups. I see their point, but to the plaintiffs, merit as expressed by grades and test scores moots such considerations.

It's a complicated question. When affirmative action policies were first implemented, there was an underlying expectation that perceived common good would outweigh personal ambition. To integrate institutions with histories of white preference, some white students were expected to forfeit privilege in the name of equity. Now some Asian Americans (who may themselves be the children of immigrants or refugees) balk at the same expectation being applied to students with very different histories.

Racial diversity on campus is visible. Students' comfort and belonging are some of the compelling reasons to promote it. But there is far more racial than wealth diversity at Harvard, and that truth doesn't figure much into discussions of affirmative action. Elite institutions overwhelmingly serve the wealthy. A 2017 study by the Equality of Opportunity Project showed that thirty-eight colleges (including five Ivy League schools) had more students from the top 1 percent than the bottom 60 percent.[8] Only 3 percent of Harvard students come from the lowest 20 percent of income distribution. As it happens, this is the same proportion of students who come from the highest one-tenth of 1 percent of the income ladder.[9] Harvard has taken steps to reduce this disparity. Families with less than $65,000 in household income pay no tuition; this affects about 20 percent of enrolled students. But the student population still skews wealthy. Average family income at Harvard is five times the general national average; well over half the students come from the top tenth of earners.

If elite schools wanted to change the picture to one of greater inclusion, they could enlarge the number of students in each incoming class. They can certainly afford it. While the total number of high school graduates has grown by 44 percent in the last thirty years, Ivy League colleges grew by only 14 percent. An argument can be made for the value of attending elite schools, but the possibility is steadily shrinking as a smaller percentage of applicants are admitted each year based on criteria that consistently preserve preferred types of exclusivity.

Stick around long enough and virtually all social arrangements seem normal, even natural. One of the great things about human beings is our ability to adjust as reality shifts. Sadly, though, we are just as good at normalizing absurdity and injustice as, say, technological advancement. Years ago, working on a consulting project in rural South Carolina, I saw a collection of artifacts from local Jewish families, including Haggadot—the small books that guide the order of service on Passover. The central theme of that holiday is the liberation from slavery of the Jews under Moses' leadership. Jews were the smallest southern slaveholding population, in 1830 comprising a fraction of 1 percent of slaveholders. Still, there were some. I tried to imagine how their seders had unfolded, with diners offering gratitude and praise for their own liberation even as those they had enslaved cleared plates and poured wine.

This is just one example of the human proclivity to adjust to contradiction to the point of absurdity, of outrage. The meaning, function, and value of formal education as revealed by elite college admissions is another.

Rigging the Rankings

Parents and students rely on many things in choosing schools for application, but one guide, *everyone knows,* is thought to be fair and reliable. *U.S. News & World Report* has been releasing college and university rankings for three decades. (No longer publishing as a magazine, the corporation is in the bests business, ranking countries, states, communities, and more.) The rankings matter greatly to many institutions because parent, student, donor, and faculty choices may be influenced by them.

Numerous factors are incorporated into these rankings: graduation and retention rates, academic reputation, faculty resources, student selectivity, financial resources, alumni giving, and more. Forty percent of a school's rank depends on how many students remain in school and graduate within six years. Many institutions may be grouped at the same rank, having arrived there by different routes, depending on their populations, endowments, and other factors.

What is termed "undergraduate academic reputation" accounts for 20 percent of a school's ranking. College presidents, provosts, and admissions deans are asked to use a one-to-five scale to rate institutions in their categories (e.g., liberal arts colleges, national universities, business programs, etc.). This is termed a "peer assessment survey." There is no guarantee that those providing scores have a depth of exposure to or even acquaintance with the institutions they categorize; it appears many have little or no direct experience with schools that are distant or very different in character from their own.

In recent years, as people scrutinized the ranking process, its biases became more evident. For example, schools that have a lower acceptance rate (i.e., schools with many applicants and many rejections) rank higher, as do schools with the highest graduation rates. Both factors put schools such as historically Black colleges at a disadvantage, as they are more challenged to retain students and tend to invest in increasing enrollment rather than making it more exclusive. Having a high level of financial resources per student raises the ranking, a stumbling block for schools with smaller endowments and operating budgets. Small class sizes and high faculty pay raise rankings.

In sum, schools with large endowments, high test scores, high national profiles, and students from high-income families top the charts. In 2020, Williams, Amherst, and Swarthmore led the rankings for liberal arts colleges. Williams, with just over two thousand undergraduates, was the largest of these. Princeton, Harvard, and Columbia were the top three in the national universities category. No historically Black school popped up till Howard University appeared at number 80. There wasn't another until Hampton University, at number 217.

In July 2021, for his podcast *Revisionist History,* Malcolm Gladwell worked with statisticians and computer scientists at Reed College in Oregon (number 63 among national liberal arts colleges) to delve into the ranking system, exploring how changing key inputs would alter scores. They chose Dillard University, in New Orleans, as an example (number 22 among historically Black colleges and universities, number 171–221 among national liberal arts colleges). The statistical challenge was simple because of easy-to-spot correlations—for example, a single factor, the size of a school's endowment, was an accurate predictor of its ranking. Having a large number of students from high-income families was also determinative. And so on.

What the rankings assess most effectively is the equation of privilege and academic excellence. So far, exposing this hasn't had noticeable effect, maybe because it comes as little surprise that the richest schools rank highest. Almost everything I have written about here reinforces the same equation.

Smearing Public Spending

How did things arrive at this pass, where wealth surpasses all other factors in shaping institutions, including education? Here is one illustrative story.

In 1978, voters in California passed Proposition 13, "the People's Initiative to Limit Property Taxation," amending the state's constitution. The core change was to set the maximum property tax at 1 percent of the property's cash value. It also stipulated that increases in the assessed value of property were not to exceed 2 percent per year. The initial property assessment—the anchor for the legislation—was at its 1976 value. The amendment also required a two-thirds majority of both houses of the state legislature to raise taxes in the future, including income taxes.

The campaign is considered the first major salvo in what came to be called the "taxpayer revolt." I can't know precisely why two out of three voters favored the initiative, but its authors ran a vivid, angry campaign, stoking resentment of government and stimulating taxpayers' aversion to public spending, widely denounced as taking hard-earned money from their pockets to give to the undeserving.

The impact was huge and multidimensional. Ever since, when home ownership changes in California, a property may be reassessed at market value. One result is an enormous gap in property tax liability, with longtime home owners paying very low taxes and subsequent buyers far more. The house I grew up in, which my family bought in the early fifties, is assessed at less than $100,000; down the block, similar houses that have recently changed hands are assessed at more than $1.5 million.

Total property taxes statewide declined by 60 percent the year after Proposition 13 passed. A major impact was to reduce education spending, 60 percent of which had previously been supported by property tax revenues. When I went to public school in California, the consensus was that the state's education system was one of the best. Since 1978, the decline has been marked, reaching a point of severity that led to another referendum in 1988 mandating minimum state spending on public education.

I was engaged in 1978 to study the impact of Proposition 13 on community-based arts in California. At the time, the state's community college system was considered excellent as an educational offering and as a pathway to a four-year college. Because of generous state funding, it was also a beloved cultural resource for Californians, with concert and lecture series and other public programs not limited to enrolled students. By asking shell-shocked arts programmers at community colleges, I discovered that all such programs had ended overnight. Proposition 13 set the system on a new path, one that emphasized vocational education and practical business courses such as computer how-tos while jettisoning or de-emphasizing things like arts and humanities. These days, there are lots of hobby-type classes to attract revenue from fee-paying continuing education fans, but the concerts, lectures, and public programs have never returned to their earlier levels. Remember that mother who was scolded for buying her kids ice cream with food stamps? That scold is now in charge.

Lionizing Business

Voters' decision to reduce their own contributions to California's common welfare—such as paying taxes to support education even if one has no family members in school—seems a clear antecedent for the attitude that education is a profit center rather than a public good. I doubt that most voters who supported Proposition 13 saw themselves as foot soldiers in a revolution that would propel Ronald Reagan into the presidency. But other observers may have.

I'm thinking of a historical marker that ought to be better known: a confidential memo to the leadership of the U.S. Chamber of Commerce, authored in 1971 by soon-to-be Supreme Court Justice Lewis Powell (nominated by Richard Nixon), entitled "Attack on American Free Enterprise System."[10]

Powell spelled out what he perceived as an "assault on the enterprise system . . . from perfectly respectable elements of society: from the college campus, the pulpit, the media, the intellectual and literary journals, the arts and sciences, and from politicians." Powell condemned the ideas taught in colleges, singling out influences he found pernicious, such as Ralph Nader, Herbert Marcuse, or Charles Reich, whose book *The Greening of America* was then influential. He urged business to "conduct guerrilla warfare with those who propagandize against the system, seeking insidiously and constantly to sabotage it." He called on the U.S. Chamber of Commerce to lead the charge, exhorting readers to such actions as supporting pro-business scholarship, establishing a pro-business speakers' bureau, evaluating textbooks for objectionable ideas, demanding equal time among speakers on campus, pressing for faculty "balance," working with business schools to promote the market system, finding pro-business scholars to place essays in journals—in short, investing substantially in academic intellectual infrastructure he hoped would ensure that higher education would promote corporate values.

Powell advocated the same types of interventions in secondary education, as well as monitoring television broadcasts, stepping up political activity, and more. Knowledgeable observers draw a direct line between his 1971 call to arms and the creation of the well-financed network of right-wing think tanks (such as the Heritage Foundation) that have had so much influence in the educational and political arenas Powell mentioned.

What does it mean to be educated? To Powell, the Chamber of Commerce, and the other institutional supporters of his campaign to eliminate threats to market domination of public life, it meant to be sure favored ideas are well funded and

ideas that threaten their preferred social order are denounced, stigmatized, and pressured into submission. It may be tempting to see the seventies' "taxpayer revolt" as somehow spontaneous, expressing organic public will. But really it is just one manifestation of the massive propaganda project Powell ignited, declaring markets to be the most admirable part of the U.S. system and devaluing social goods that don't turn a profit.

Among people involved in community-based arts, anyone of a certain age is bound to remember holding a CETA job (the Comprehensive Employment and Training Act of 1973 enabled this public service employment program much beloved by community artists) or being close to people who did. Eliminating these public service jobs was one of the first things Reagan did after his inauguration. Although funding for community-based arts work was never easy or abundant, veterans of that period see a clear dividing line in time, pre- and post-Reagan, before and after a sustainable consensus on the value of social goods that had lasted since FDR. Eisenhower, a Republican, warned against the "military-industrial complex." Nixon, a Republican, proposed a guaranteed annual income. Once Reagan took office, nearly a decade into the pro-business domination Powell called for, imagining a Republican advocating such things became impossible. And the people whose right to life, liberty, and the pursuit of happiness could not be secured in the marketplace became collateral damage.

Buyer's Remorse

To the denizens of higher education, what does it mean to be educated? During the pandemic, some answers came to light when students and parents positioned themselves as consumers of overpriced or fraudulent goods.

At quite a few colleges, students (graduate students in particular) petitioned—even sued—for tuition refunds. Most schools had already reimbursed fees for dining and housing that students could not use under quarantine conditions. School leaders understood campus closures as mandatory rather than resulting from cost-benefit calculation or other choice. Faculty and administrators were asked to take on a good deal of extra work to support students and make the transition to online learning. This was taxing for art schools, for instance, which had to find ways to teach subjects such as ceramics and glass without access to studio and workshop space.

Many of the students who protested were facing very real economic challenges. For low-income students, having to move to off-campus housing and meals and having to replace work space and equipment could be prohibitive. The sense of being cheated by the pandemic was real and widespread, extending far beyond higher education. But the protests and suits also revealed that many students and their parents saw higher education as a consumer-provider relationship: *I paid for this and all I got was that! You owe me!*

Most such lawsuits were rejected by judges on the grounds that courts cannot rule on the quality of education; after all, students were still enrolled, still taking part online, still obtaining grades and credits. To proceed, suits would have to show there was some breach of promise, which might be assessed by comparing what was pledged in promotional materials and enrollment documents with what was provided. In some cases, the fact that colleges had offered online classes before the pandemic—and charged less for them than for in-person classes—was deemed germane. One idea behind the refund demands was that colleges' facilities expense and related costs dropped once classes were no longer held on campus, so a larger portion of fees accrued to the institution, an accidental benefit that should be shared with students. With respect to the small number of lawsuits that stood, a few colleges have settled, calculating that the costs entailed would be far lower than the costs of taking the cases to court.

The many examples of higher education being treated like a business transaction, from choosing an institution understood to promise the largest postgraduation salaries to demanding reimbursement on account of pandemic conditions, suggest that education is often seen mainly as a means to a practical end.

As a thought experiment, take money out of the equation. What does it mean to be educated? To me, an autodidact, to be educated means studying inherited knowledge, cultivating awareness, embracing curiosity, nurturing personal and social imagination, and always questioning orthodoxy. It means developing the qualities of heart and mind that prepare one to be as agile as possible whatever life may bring, including disappointments. It doesn't mean anything in particular about my financial condition.

What does it mean to you?

The Uncolonized Mind

In my angel portraits, I dubbed Paul Goodman "The Angel of the Uncolonized Mind." Many intellectuals emerge from formal training with minds accustomed to what Rabbi Abraham Joshua Heschel (another of my angels) called "notions," conventional ideas that are more or less immune to scrutiny, that are merely accepted as fixed stars in the cultural firmament. With almost everyone crediting certain ideas as true, it is easy for minds to become colonized by a way of seeing that constrains perception and vision.

Heschel's desire to awaken us focused on truly conventional ideas, lazy notions that slip into belief without friction. That is how mind colonization starts. But today it has taken on a new and even more insidious aspect. As if in speeded-up footage, we see decidedly fringe ideas being midwifed into acceptance by a cascade—an avalanche—of well-orchestrated exhortations from widely read but unverified sources such as white supremacist websites and social media accounts. It's not as if these ideas are novel. To the contrary, their messages have been resounding for generations: that privilege is deserved, that its loss is injury, that powerful hidden enemies are putting civilization itself at risk. With shrewd propaganda watering seeds that were planted generations ago, in record time bizarre notions grow into truths that *everyone knows.*

Mind colonization is a communicable disease, one I dread catching. When people cede room in their minds to conventional notions, I want passionately to question orthodoxies, to allow thought experiments free rein, to make every attempt to see what has been obscured by colonized thought. This choice isn't presented very clearly in the annals of formal education, but for me it is the most central and definitive choice of all when I ask "What does it mean to be educated?"

For too many (but thankfully by no means all) of those engaged in providing formal education—teaching, planning curriculum, administering institutions—education appears to mean imparting existing knowledge. Whether the education in question follows a technical model, conveying the information and skills one needs to run a public library, say, or casts the net more widely to scoop in an authorized history of philosophy or aesthetics, what my beloved angel Paulo Freire called "banking education," in which information is deposited as coins into a bank, predominates.

In contrast, the most valuable educational approach to prepare one for living fully is to teach students to see their own values, assumptions, and beliefs clearly, then to explore a wide-ranging history of thought and action to discover which of these are truly sound, truly worth living by.

The uncolonized mind is perpetually alive to questions, discovering and testing alternatives to received knowledge. The uncolonized mind may experience the discouragements society puts in its path—be careful about proposing controversial ideas, don't make waves, don't question constituted authority—but will always decide that freedom of thought matters more. All of my angels, the people who have inspired me most, valued the uncolonized mind enough to risk inhabiting it.

Engaging the Quadruple Pandemic

How might the experience of formal education change if the wall between credentialed expertise and lived knowledge came down?

From the spring of 2020 on, I thought of our national predicament as a quadruple pandemic: COVID-19, the racial violence that catalyzed Black Lives Matter and the pushback that followed, escalating climate crisis, and the accompanying economic disaster. How to respond has been framed repeatedly as a choice: Go back to "normal" or recognize a wake-up call when it resounds, then move into new ways of living.

It's an epic choice, terribly complicated by the differing fortunes of various sectors in a time of trial. Many of the largest corporations and wealthiest individuals became even wealthier during the period of greatest suffering, risk, and constriction for others. The system worked for them, and their clout with policymakers and private-sector forces helped to shape our collective direction. For ordinary people, especially those in minimum-wage jobs or out of work altogether, deprivation and fear have often been overwhelming.

To the extent that it may offer a space for study, reflection, and innovation, formal education has a unique opportunity in such times: to welcome people in, to use formidable resources to engage possible futures. If I were teaching right now, I would attempt to see our shared situation through the lens of the uncolonized mind. With that awareness, my driving intentions would be two.

First, I would want to invite students to take an encompassing look at where we are as a society, employing the masses of data and stories now available, using creative methods to dig deeper, bringing students into contact not just with faculty and one another but also with people outside the academy who can help to achieve a fuller picture of reality.

Then I would want to enlarge the circle of dialogue to engage as many people as possible who have visions of possible futures—whether dystopian or encouraging—to assist students in devising scenarios. Who stands to gain and lose in each scenario? How would the distribution of power and resources be affected by each? What possible roles exist for people like themselves in each scenario? For those whose gifts or circumstances are very different? What social structures, methods, and approaches would be required to enable each scenario? What obstacles stand in the way of each?

Individual students would gain a broad perspective, bringing a world of knowledge to bear on a truly worthy challenge. Faculty would have compelling reasons to cross discipline lines and collaborate, as opposed to a situation in which interdisciplinarity sounds attractive but somewhat abstract. It would also help students answer a question of personal import. Would such exploration suggest a meaningful path toward the future each student desires?

This type of inquiry and imagination would weaken higher education's ramparts, eroding exclusivity with participatory methods. In the sphere I know best, there is a vibrant field of participatory public art in which people from a community where work is to be sited contribute their experiences and visions to a mural or sculpture park or installation. Oral history-based literature and theater use people's direct experience to devise a resonant collective story. Just so, the testimonies of culture bearers and culture builders who cannot be on campus in person could be experienced online or through video and audio recordings.

This would be a radical re-envisioning of formal education for a radically different time. Although it would diverge significantly from time-honored curriculum, it would be able to draw fully on the knowledge and wisdom of the past. I love the way the French human rights activist Francis Jeanson put this in his definition of cultural democracy, a concept central to my work: "[I]ts aim is to arrange things in such a way that culture becomes today for everybody what culture was for a small number of privileged people at every stage of history where it succeeded in reinventing for the benefit of the living the legacy inherited from the dead."

Is this not the essential task of education? This invitation has guided my own self-education, freeing me to range widely and look deeply. I can't find a way to improve it.

15

Ask The Angels

I took my dilemma to the studio, hoping once again that the angels would shed some light.

"Friends," I began, "can I call you friends?"

"We've been spending quite a bit of time together," said James Baldwin. No one demurred.

"Okay, then," I said. "I need some perspective. Things are kind of crazy. Many people are in the grip of conspiracy theories. Not long ago, a mob stormed the national Capitol, egged on by the outgoing president, who continually spreads the false belief that the 2020 presidential election was stolen. When children are massacred in schools—this has happened more often than you may want to believe—large groups of people claim it is a hoax carried out by actors; they harass the bereaved parents. During the 2016 election campaign, a man opened fire on an ordinary pizza restaurant, having been convinced that politicians used it as a front for sex trafficking of children. There are vast and bizarre stories—one is called QAnon, perpetrated by Q, a mysterious figure who has since disap-

peared, but there are always others to take his place. What they have in common is the conviction that powerful behind-the-scenes figures are controlling things, a clandestine triumph of world domination, and that only a few of us have realized this."

"I have heard that story before," said Abraham Joshua Heschel. "I would not be surprised if many of them were blaming us."

"Some are," I said. "But by no means just us. It's much stranger than that. Have you heard of simulation theory?"

Only John Trudell had. "Is this life a dream? Am I dreaming it? Is it dreaming me? The ancients asked these questions," he said. "Also *The Matrix*."

"That's a film," I explained to the rest, "a moving picture that says our consensus reality is an illusion created by superintelligent machines that have taken over the world. They have devised elaborate methods of deceiving us into not knowing that we are actually passive energy sources plugged into an enormous grid—"

"*Un moment,*" said Henri de Toulouse-Lautrec. "A little slower, please."

139

"It's hard to imagine, I know," I continued. "It's fantastic. What if our existence is a dream others have created, a dream that replaces real life? While our bodies lie motionless, stacked like cordwood, being drained of energy to feed our masters, we believe ourselves to be freely moving about the world, going about our ordinary lives."

"*Comme* Jules Verne?" asked Lautrec.

"In a way," I said. "Only instead of journeying under the sea or to the moon, humans are imprisoned, but we don't know it because we are fed simulated experience. In the film and its sequels, a few awaken, escape, and rebel. Some people say this is not just a movie, that it's a faithful rendering of our true condition."

"Plato's 'Allegory of the Cave,'" said Isaiah Berlin. "We believe we are encountering the world, but we are trapped in shadows."

"Do you believe any of these tales?" asked Doris Lessing. "The bit about simulation theory or the Q thing? I wrote space fictions sometimes, but they, too, were allegories."

"No, I don't. But here's my dilemma," I said. "In these stories, the villains are actually the vilified—Black people, Asians, Jews, Muslims, sexual minorities, and so on. I can't begin to believe any of these loony tunes, but I sometimes think they have so much appeal because they hold exactly one grain of truth. Take away the scapegoating and it's there: Things have been rigged to benefit those who believe they deserve to rule over the rest. The way popular conspiracy theories are framed, it's a noxious twist: They exist to distract or placate the people who might otherwise notice who is really exploiting them."

"The conspiracies you describe are ridiculous, fever dreams of the paranoid. But underneath all the fantasy, the story is only a little off, isn't it?" asked Paul Goodman. "Powerful, if not invisible, forces are indeed ruling through social structures and processes created for their own benefit. They do a fairly good job of convincing the less powerful that it's all well and good, just the natural order of things. This was true in my day, and given what you are saying, more true now."

"But many aren't convinced," said Nina Simone. "Look at the civil rights struggles. Look at how many of my people are doing all they can to awaken the world to injustice and change things."

"More now than in my time," agreed Baldwin, "or so I hear."

"I like to think it's an inflection point," I told them, "a crossroads. Conspiracies imagined and promulgated by the far right are gaining traction. Elected officials promote them and are doing all they can to deprive their opponents of the vote, to secure a permanent hold on the instruments of government. But Jimmy is right." I looked at Baldwin. "Can I call you Jimmy?" He nodded. "The resistance is enormous, and from what I've seen, very few of its members would disagree that the system is rigged to benefit the privileged. I hope we still have a choice, that there are enough of us to defeat the authoritarians."

"Of course there's a choice," said Lessing. "But if things resemble my time, many people may be afraid to make it."

"Or if not afraid," said Jane Jacobs, "just so used to the way things are, so convinced of their dependence on the system—as

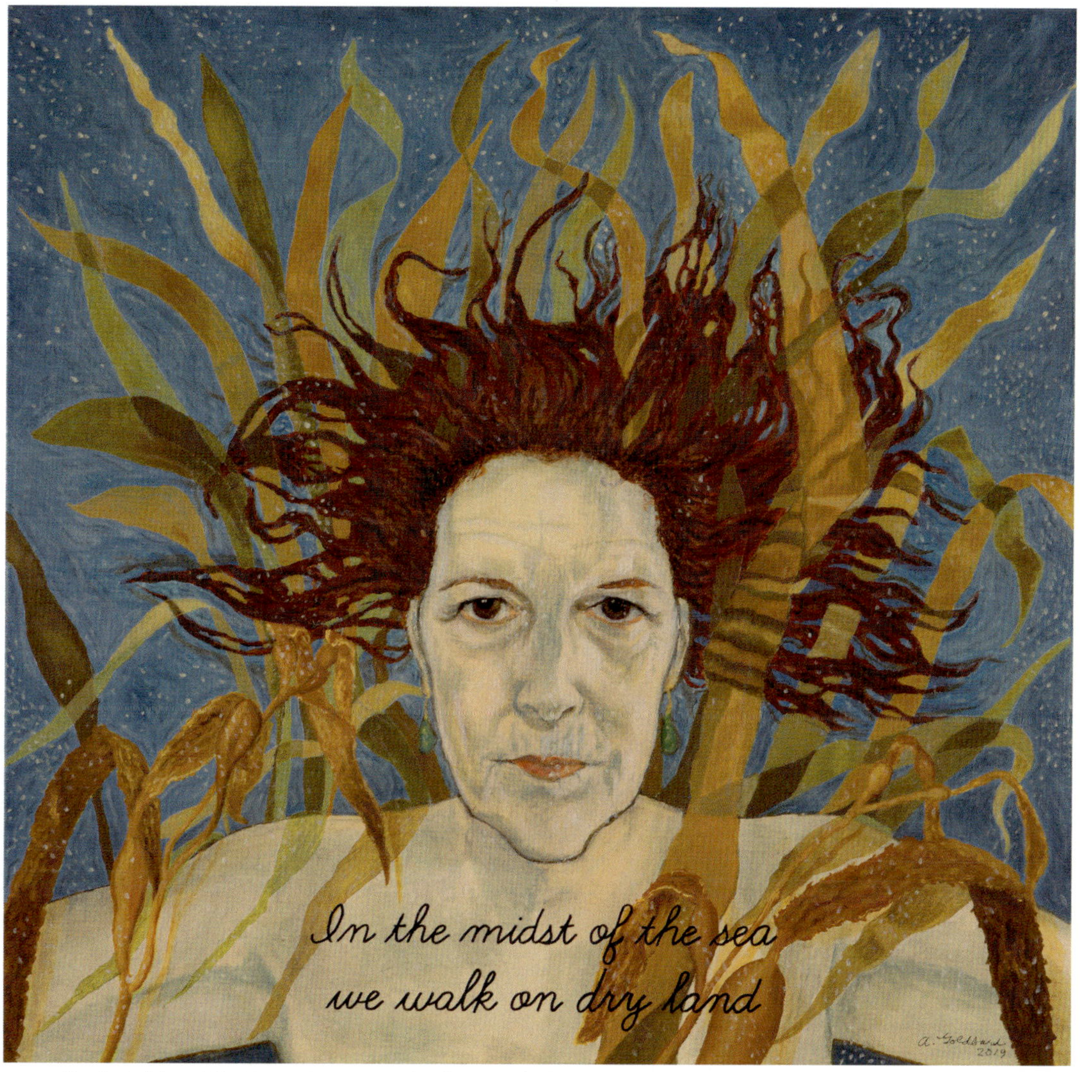

"In the Midst of the Sea," 24 x 24 inch oil on panel from the 2019 series, "Gaia and Shekhina Speak."

Senhor Freire said—that they've come to believe there is no alternative."

"Call me Paulo, please. This is internalization of the oppressor," Paulo Freire said. "Exactly. After so much insistence and repetition, people become convinced that this social order is right and good. It must be rescued from its enemies. They align with those who actually scorn them and against those who suffer."

"When the first *Matrix* came out," said Trudell, "people were posting quotes from the character Morpheus all the time. 'You have to understand,' he said, 'most of these people are not ready to be unplugged. And many of them are so inured, so hopelessly dependent on the system that they will fight to protect it.'"

"Okay, I get it," said Simone. "I'm trying to wrap my head around what it would have been like if people in my time believed life was a simulation. A nightmare, maybe."

"I don't think there are many of them," I told her. "The movie is just a handy way to describe the level of credulity. But quite a few do believe the pizza conspiracy and the stolen election and QAnon and much more, and they are everywhere. If you were alive today, you would encounter them all the time."

"I still have a question," said Alice Neel. "If what you say is true—and it sounds true to me, by the way—why are you so worked up over this credentials thing, Arlene? Is that the worst of it?"

"I was going to ask something like that," said Lautrec. "In my time, there were men in starched collars or officers' uniforms who thought they were put on earth to keep everyone else in their place. Most of us ignored them and went about our business. Do you really think Montmartre cared what they thought?"

"Montmartre cared more than you might have imagined," Lessing said, "once the German occupation started in 1940. But who can imagine the world forty years after one's death? I died only a decade ago, and I am straining to comprehend the world of today as Arlene describes it."

"Exactly," I said. "It beggars imagination. But you are right, Ms. Neel—"

"Please, Alice."

"You are right, Alice." I smiled. "Many people are claiming that what they care about takes precedence, and they care about huge, wicked problems: climate crisis, racial justice, women's rights, wealth disparity, homophobia, religious bigotry, imperialism. . . . I can't disagree with any of them. To me, it's all connected. I can't wrap my mind around these climate deniers. Do they really delude themselves that their children will able to buy their way into safety on a burning planet? Do these people really think the world in which women are forced to bear unwanted children will be a hospitable place for their children's daughters if, God forbid, they are raped? Do they imagine a private bucolic future while armed militias occupy city streets, terrorizing people of color who dare to stand for even the most basic human rights? To me, it is all part of the same thing, the drive for domination by the few broken and bloated egos at the expense of everyone else. And all of it can be measured with the same yardstick: *Cui bono?*"

"Who benefits?" said Berlin. "Often quoted more than two thousand years ago by the Roman statesman Cicero, who attributed it to Lucius Cassius, and still an excellent question."

"All of those issues are woven into a fabric of domination," I told them. "Pull on any thread and you tug at them all. There are clear beneficiaries of each oppression, and none of them is thinking far enough ahead to see that the benefits won't last. This book's little piece of the puzzle— my hope that if readers look at the class prejudices and self-dealing, the elite systems and exclusionary structures that add up to treating so many people as negligible, dispensable—I'd like to think it's just one of many doorways to reality. Wherever you start, follow the trail of beneficiaries and you'll find them all. Any doorway can lead to awakening."

"Awakening from the Matrix?" asked Trudell. "I heard someone called it 'the Patrix.'"

"I like that," said Neel and Simone in unison.

"I just want us—the still living—to remember who we are," I said. "Not angels like you, but flesh and blood, with far more potential to heal our societies than those who have anointed themselves our masters want us to believe. I want to share what I learned from you as teachers."

"Last time we talked, we granted permission to quote ourselves." Heschel looked around, seeing no objections. "You are reminding me of something I wrote. 'There is an evil which most of us condone and are even guilty of: indifference to evil. We remain neutral, impartial, and not easily moved by the wrongs done unto other people. Indifference to evil is more insidious than evil itself; it is more universal, more contagious, more dangerous. A silent justification, it makes possible an evil erupting as an exception becoming the rule and being in turn accepted.' I wrote that for the conference on race and religion in 1963. That's where I met my friend Martin of blessed memory, Dr. King."

"You are describing one of my aims in writing about my neighbors," Jacobs explained. "A doorway. I didn't think paving over our neighborhood and destroying our space for conviviality was the worst thing they could do to us. I just thought it was the next thing. I thought it was something people could grasp, a lived reality, not a dream."

"In one way, it's a simple challenge," Baldwin said. "Just take the pattern of these conspiracies and transfer them to what can be proven—who's in charge, what they gain but also lose, how everyone helps or hinders them."

"Simple isn't easy," said Simone.

"Easy isn't everything," said Goodman.

The studio became very quiet.

Encountering Your Angels

The process of identifying and honoring my angels—the people whose work shaped my own worldview and ideas—was profound and illuminating for me. I hope you will want to try it, too.

There are so many people I admire, so many from whom I've learned. When I began this series of portraits, I wondered how to choose. A few were clear from the first. I began by painting James Baldwin, certain there was no way someone whose beauty and influence so astounded me could be left off the list. Then I set the parameters for my remaining choices. If you want to encounter your angels to learn more about both them and yourself, your task is to do the same. (If the angel metaphor doesn't work for you, feel free to substitute guides, teachers, or any word you like.)

While my first angel painting was in process, I chose a few guidelines for the rest. They had to be human beings and deceased. No restrictions as to age, time period, ethnicity, gender, location, or any other such category. I like the idea of a manageable number. I set out to paint a minyan of ten, but the total crept up to eleven. I began the process thinking this was a personal project, a private one. But once the paintings emerged, memoirs and essays materialized to make this book.

What would your parameters be?

Honor

How will you identify your angels, the specific individuals you wish to honor for their roles in shaping your life? The first step I suggest is inquiry, focusing on a question I have posed many times in this book:

What does it mean to be educated? What does it mean to *you*?

Try to open a line of fearless inquiry into the true sources of your character, knowledge, skill, and wisdom. Formal schooling is likely to be one of them, perhaps even the main one. But it is highly unlikely to be the only one. A few questions may help you complete your list:

Recall times when encountering someone's thinking or action called your own assumptions into question, sparking a radical rethinking, changing your relationship to something important in your life. Who catalyzed a turning point?

Who has inspired you and how?

What are the sources of your own salient qualities, the ones familiar to people who know you well?

I suggest spending some time with your list before it is finalized. You may come up with a long list you want to narrow; or wake up one morning astounded to realize whom you left out. To me, the most important question is whom you wish to honor. Each angel should be an answer.

Naming came next for me, because it helped me hone in on the specific character of the honor I wished to convey. I chose "the Camp of Angels of Freedom" for my collective name because freedom is of utmost importance to me. Naming the individuals followed from that. For the first part of each name, I picked a word or phrase that expressed the essence of my relationship to that figure. For the second part, I picked a quality that person embodied.

A visual representation is important, something you find or make that is large enough to post and live with, even if temporarily. The images will create a kind of shrine to your angels, enabling you to be in their presence. I made paintings, but you can download, draw, or collage an image, whatever works to remind you who your teachers are.

Gratitude

Honor comes with gratitude, or what good is it? You know what you are grateful for, and you'll find a way to express it. For me, it was very helpful to hang my angel images around a room. Encountering each image helped me offer gratitude in a commensurate form, which might be words of thanks, a bow, a literal offering such as incense or flowers, a blessing.

I was driven by the desire to create something that embodied my feelings toward each angel. For me, that led to paintings and essays. If you wish, you could create a dance, a poem, a piece of music, a monologue, a collage—or just be aware of your own thoughts and feelings.

I've found myself entering into a dialogue with my angels. Sometimes I wondered what more I must do to fully integrate what one person taught me. I can also imagine asking for help with a dilemma. My method is simple: open my heart and invite a reply to arise in my mind. Accuracy is a trap best avoided; there is no way to be certain what a faraway or no longer living person would say or do. To me, it's best to gratefully accept whatever comes to you.

Reflection

Most important for me has been to reflect on what I have learned. Do the lessons of each angel offer a new understanding I want to integrate? Do they invite any type of fresh inquiry?

This process could be powerful in parallel with a partner, coming together for reflection. The insight possible, even into the inner world of someone you know very well, is likely to be surprising, just as is the self-insight you will gain.

Endnotes

Chapter 13

1. National Center for Education Statistics, "Status and Trends in the Education of Racial and Ethnic Groups, Indicator 23: Postsecondary Graduation Rates," February 2019, https://neces.ed.gov/.

2. Stephanie Saul and Anemona Hartocollis, "Lawsuit Says 16 Elite Colleges Are Part of Price-Fixing Cartel," *New York Times,* January 10, 2022, www.nytimes.com.

3. Marty Ahrens and Ben Evarts, *Natural Gas and Propane Fires, Explosions and Leaks Estimates and Incident Descriptions* (Quincy, MA: National Fire Protection Association, 2018), *3.*

4. Daniel Byman, "Some Good News from 2020: So Far, Very Few Americans Have Been Killed in Terrorist Attacks," *Washington Post,* December 21, 2020, www.washingtonpost.com.

5. Daniel Byman, "2021 Saw Plenty of Violence—but No Mass Terrorist Attacks in the U.S.," *Washington Post,* December 29, 2021, www.washingtonpost.com.

Chapter 14

1. Akintunde Ahmad, "The Bleak Truth Behind My 'Inspiring' Path from Oakland to Yale," *The Atlantic,* September 12, 2019, www.theatlantic.com.

2. Farran Powell, Emma Kerr, and Sarah Wood, "See the Average College Tuition in 2021–2022," *U.S. News & World Report,* September 13, 2021, www.usnews.com/education.

3. Timothy Bella, "A Professor Said Her Students Think Americans Make Six Figures on Average. That's a Long Way Off," *Washington Post,* January 20, 2022, www.washingtonpost.com.

4. Laura Pappano, "The Master's as the New Bachelor's," *New York Times,* July 22, 2011, www.nytimes.com.

5. Jon Marcus, "More High School Grads Than Ever Are Going to College, but 1 in 5 Will Quit," *The Hechinger Report,* July 5, 2018, https://hechingerreport.org/.

6. Peter Coy, "Wealth Inequality Is the Highest Since World War II," *New York Times,* February 2, 2022, www.nytimes.com.

7. Peter Arcidiacono, Josh Kinsler, and Tyler Ransom, "Legacy and Athlete Preferences at Harvard," NBER Working Paper No. 26316, September 2019.

8. Jeffrey J. Selingo, "Harvard and Its Peers Should Be Embarrassed about How Few Students They Educate," *Washington Post,* April 8, 2021, www.washington post.com.

9. Daniel Friedman, "Opportunity at Harvard," Harvard Open Data Project, February 28, 2020, https://medium.com/harvard-open-data-project.

10. Lewis Powell, "The Powell Memo (also known as the Powell Manifesto)," August 23, 1971, Reclaim Democracy, https://reclaim democracy.org.

Acknowledgments

I am so grateful to the readers who reviewed various drafts and sections of this book and offered their wise guidance: Larry Bogad, Betty Farrell, Amber Hansen, Bill Lazar, François Matarasso, Judith Marcuse, Lynn Rosen, Marc Weiss, and Rick Yoshimoto. Whatever works here is owing to their care. All errors are my own.

Many thanks to Molly Wagoner of Blue Koru Photoworks in Santa Fe for photographing the angel portraits, and to Rick Yoshimoto for photographing my self-portraits.

About the Author

Arlene Goldbard is a writer, visual artist, speaker, social activist, and consultant. She and her husband, the artist Rick Yoshimoto, live just outside Santa Fe, New Mexico.

Arlene's essays have appeared in many journals and anthologies. Her books include *Crossroads: Reflections on the Politics of Culture; New Creative Community: The Art of Cultural Development; Community, Culture and Globalization; The Culture of Possibility: Art, Artists & the Future;* and her novels, *Clarity* and *The Wave.*

Arlene has offered hundreds of talks and workshops and helped many organizations make plans and solve problems. They include nonprofits such as the Independent Television Service, the National Campaign for Freedom of Expression, and the New Museum of Contemporary Art; foundations such as the Rockefeller Foundation and the Paul Robeson Fund for Independent Media; a score of state arts agencies; and many others.

Until 2019, she served as Chief Policy Wonk of the U.S. Department of Arts and Culture and president of the Board of Directors of The Shalom Center.

Many of her talks, essays, and paintings can be found on her website, www.arlenegoldbard.com, where you can also subscribe to her blog.